Your Scripture
for Today

Your Scripture for Today

For All
Who Are
Blessed
to Be
a Blessing!

Kim Batchelder

YOUR SCRIPTURE FOR TODAY
FOR ALL WHO ARE BLESSED TO BE A BLESSING!

iUniverse books may be ordered through booksellers or by contacting:

iUniverse
1663 Liberty Drive
Bloomington, IN 47403
www.iuniverse.com
1-800-Authors (1-800-288-4677)

Because of the dynamic nature of the Internet, any web addresses or links contained in this book may have changed since publication and may no longer be valid. The views expressed in this work are solely those of the author and do not necessarily reflect the views of the publisher, and the publisher hereby disclaims any responsibility for them.

Any people depicted in stock imagery provided by Thinkstock are models, and such images are being used for illustrative purposes only. Certain stock imagery © Thinkstock.

ISBN: 978-1-4917-7375-8 (sc)
ISBN: 978-1-4917-7374-1 (e)

Library of Congress Control Number: 2015912933

Print information available on the last page.

iUniverse rev. date: 9/18/2015

Contents

Introduction

When I think about my journey and the fact that I am writing this introduction to a book that I know has totally been inspired by God, I am in awe of His majesty. You hear others say do what you love and it will not feel like work. Well the compilation of writings in the next pages was done because of my love for God's word and my love for sharing His word with others. I believe we are all called according to His purpose and I believe my purpose is to give bite sized pieces of the word of God so that it's easy to digest, but sticks with you throughout the day.

God gave me the desire to send out a Scripture each day initially in 1997 in Detroit, MI at my place of employment. I wanted to give everyone the gift of the word every morning, so I would write the book, chapter, and verse on a sticking note and place it on the computers in the morning because I arrived earlier than most. My hope was that they would take that sticky note home with the scripture on it, look it up and study it. Upon relocating to Houston, Texas in 1998 and starting my new job there I created an email list and began to send a Scripture each day in the same format as the sticky note, just online. Until one of my co-workers came to me and stated that it would be better if I typed the scripture out because it's hard to bring the bible into work and look it up. So, with that observation I began to type the scripture out and thus Your Scripture for today was born. I never thought in my wildest dreams that writing a scripture on a sticky note would be such an inspiration to so many people. Because within no time I began to receive requests to add more and more people on my list. After about a year, God led me to add a small commentary i.e. observation to the emails and that is when I added my motto "You are Blessed to be a Blessing!"

If anyone would ask what qualifies me to write a book about God's word, I would have to answer by saying, we are all called to be ministers of reconciliation and to share the good news of His word. I wish I could tell you that my years of schooling, even getting a graduate degree, gave me the qualifications to write about the goodness of God. But I can't take the credit for all the words of healing, encouragement, inspiration, enlightenment, and thanksgiving, because they are all inspired by God. I can only take the credit for being a willing vessel and being obedient to what He has called me to do! When the words of encouragement come back to me saying "How did you know I needed to hear that today", my response is always, "I didn't, but He did!"

This led me to be sitting in front of my computer typing this introduction to the book, Your Scripture for Today. It's such a blessing to be in God's mighty flow and to be in the place that God has destined me to be. I am confident that as you read the scriptures and observations each day, you will get closer to God and you will be inspired, encouraged, enlightened, thankful, and in total peace with God and with yourself! Therefore you will be open to receive all the blessings that God has for you. Just remember that as God begins to bless you turn around and bless someone else! You are blessed to be a Blessing!

Dedications

This book is dedicated to my Mom Kathlyn Pore' she was and still is my inspiration. I do miss talking with her every day but I know she is smiling down from heaven on me. Of course I also want to dedicate this book to my daughters Andrea and Brittany, Grandson Aiden and my husband Phillip for your love and support during this process.

I also want to acknowledge and thank all those who have received the "Daily Word" via email for more than 16 years. Thank you to all my family and friends who encouraged me to put them into a book. I appreciate every email you sent with encouraging words! Special thanks to Dawn, Chantele, Byron and Consuella for staying on me to get this book done!

In addition thanks to Deonte Scott for contributing the quote below to this book. As well as my Brother Pastor Daniel Pore' for the artwork on the awesome cover!

Don't let fear keep you from sowing your gift to the world!
There are many people wasting the gift that God has given
them instead of making a useful purpose out it!
Deonte Scott

JANUARY

Your scripture for today:

Ephesians 3:19

May you experience the love of Christ, though it is too great to understand fully. Then you will be made complete with all the fullness of life and power that comes from God.

Observation:

Can you imagine being filled up with God's love?

What an experience that would be! To understand how our Father operates with total compassion for others and ourselves. I believe we would truly understand what this life is about and walk in the power that God has for us. Love is the one emotion that can rule over so many things. When you show your love for another it can give them hope. When you say I love you to that special someone it can brighten their day! The more love you give out the more you will receive. God's love for you is over the top. His love is unconditional. You are His child no matter what you do he will always Love You!

You are blessed to be a Blessing!

My prayer for you is that you feel the presence and the love of God today and every day!

January 2

Your scripture for today:

Isaiah 43:18-19

Forget the former things; do not dwell on the past. See, I am doing a new thing! Now it springs up; do you not perceive it? I am making a way in the desert and streams in the wasteland.

Observation:

Welcome to a new day! It's a brand new year and you have the opportunity to start fresh. However, this all begins within you first. The situations or circumstances may still be the same but it's all about how we decide to see it. By changing the way you look at a situation it can totally change. By changing how you speak about your circumstances they can change. Instead of murmuring and complaining about how things are, take some time and visualize how you want them to be, then speak about that. When negative thoughts come to your mind, don't speak them out. Change it to a positive. When those negative, drama seekers come around, politely dismiss yourself from that environment. Seek after and surround yourself with those with positive energy. Make a decision not to sweat the small stuff and make this your best day ever.

You are blessed to be a Blessing!

My prayer for you today is that you will have the best day ever because this is the day the Lord has made. It's new just for you!

Your scripture for today:

Proverbs 13:12

**Hope deferred makes the heart sick, but when
the desire is fulfilled, it is a tree of life.**

Observation:

*Hope is the key ingredient to having faith. If you don't have anything
you are hoping for then there is no need for faith. Remember faith is the
evidence of things hoped for. When you don't have hope you can think
that life is not worth living. You may have stepped out and tried to do
something that was not different then the norm and it didn't work out.
Don't be afraid to take that step and try something new. You have to
be like that little child just learning how to walk. They get up and their
legs are shaking, they try to take one step and might fall, but they get
back up again and again until they get it! God put that same ability
in you, to take that step, fall and get back up until you get it. You were
created to be a goal-oriented visionary, so continue to hope for new
things in your life, have faith and trust that God will bring it to pass!*

You are blessed to be a Blessing!

*My prayer for you today is that whatever you desire
will come to pass because you continue to hope
for it and believe that it is already done!*

Your scripture for today:

Proverbs 12:18

**Reckless words pierce like a sword, but the
tongue of the wise brings healing.**

Observation:

*Your words can edify, bless, encourage, heal, and comfort others. On
the other hand your words can tear down, curse, wound and abuse
others. Words are like seeds, they bloom where ever they get planted.
When you speak encouraging words to a child you will see that child
grow with good healthy self-esteem and confident in his or her abilities.
When negative words have been spoken to a child they grow up with a
chip on their shoulder and feel less than others. Those seeds of verbal
abuse can be carried on from generation to generation, from childhood
to adulthood. But when you think before you speak it can make all the
difference and break the negative cycle producing a positive legacy. Be
the wise one and think about how you would want to be spoken to and
speak to others that way.*

You are blessed to be a Blessing!

*My prayer for you is that you speak positive words of
encouragement today and bring healing everywhere you go!*

January 5

Your scripture for today:

Luke 16:10

**Whoever can be trusted with very little can also be
trusted with much, and whoever is dishonest with
very little will also be dishonest with much.**

Observation:

*God wants to give you everything you want but will give you as much
as you can be trusted with. There are times that God wants to give you
your wants but because He is a good father, He will only give you what
you need. He knows when you are really ready to receive your wants.
He wants you to prosper as your soul prospers. Look to increase in the
knowledge of God. Be determined to understand the purpose for your
desires and dreams. Then when you ask for more you will handle it
better because you understand the reason God is blessing you with
it. Be good stewards over whatever you have and more is on the way.*

You are blessed to be a Blessing!

*My prayer for you today is that you increase in the knowledge of
God so that He can bless you with all that you want and need!*

Your scripture for today:

Matthew 11: 28-30

Come to me, all you who labor and are heavy laden, and I will give you rest. Take my yoke upon you and learn from me, for I am gentle and lowly in heart, and you will find rest for your souls. For my yoke is easy and my burden is light.

Observation:

If you are a parent, I am sure you have seen your child running around trying to figure things out on their own and all the while you knew exactly what they needed to get it done faster and easier. Have you ever been given an assignment to get done at work and it requires you to use a software program that you have no idea how it works? Instead of asking for help you stress yourself out trying to figure it out, when someone with that knowledge could help you get it done with ease and grace. God is always reminding us to stop running ourselves crazy. He wants you to come to him and ask for his assistance in everything you do. His ways are so much easier than what you can even think to do. All he asks is that you come to him learn from him and find the rest and peace that *you need to succeed in every area of your life.*

You are blessed to be a Blessing!

> *My prayer for you today is that you ask God to be in everything you do today. Release it and let it go.*

January 7

Your scripture for today:

Philippians 1:6

Being confident of this, that he who began a good work in you will carry it on to completion until the day of Christ Jesus.

Observation:

When you are confident about something no one can tell you anything. You are bold, determined and have courage to succeed. Believe that God has started a good work in you and he is going to finish it. He is not like man who starts things then changes his mind because of difficult times, or money looks funny, or the weather isn't perfect. No, God started it he is finishing it so just allow him to complete the project he started in you!

You are blessed to be a Blessing!

My prayer for you today is that you will be confident in the work and purpose that God has for you!

January 8

Your scripture for today:

Romans 15:4

For whatever things were written before were written for our learning, that we through the patience and comfort of the Scriptures might have hope.

Observation:

Remember that the word was written for us to learn, to get wisdom, and to understand how to live this life. It's an instruction manual that becomes clearer the more you read it and meditate on it. When the words get in you and they become alive in your spirit you begin to understand how God is leading and guiding your life. You will be encouraged by studying the word daily. Your faith will build as you see the examples of how God performed miracles in the lives of those in the Word. When you know what the word says you can apply it to your life and have more hope for the future.

You are blessed to be a Blessing!

My prayer for you today is that you will spend time meditating on God's word today!

Your scripture for today:

Joel 2:25-26

I will repay you for the years the locusts have eaten the great locust and the young locust, the other locust and locust swarm my great army that I sent among you. You will have plenty to eat, until you are full, and you will praise the name of the Lord your God, who has worked wonders for you: never again will my people be shamed.

Observation:

Whatever you have been lacking in God wants to restore it back to you. When you're feeling low He will give you joy. When you are lacking in love He will give you unconditional love. When you need peace He reminds you that you are called to peace. Maybe you don't have friends, He gives you companionship. Lacking in finances, He came to give us life and life more abundantly. It doesn't matter what it looks like. God is able to give you the big pay back! You will have an overflow of what you need. Understand that this is the year of new beginnings and God is going to repay back to you double for your trouble, just give glory to God.

You are blessed to be a Blessing!

My prayer for you today is that you receive double blessings for your trouble!

January 10

Your scripture for today:

Matthew 18:19-20

**Again, I tell you that if two of you on earth agree
about anything you ask for, it will be done for you
by my father in heaven. For where two or three come
together in my name there am I with them.**

Observation:

*The power of agreement is awesome. When you have a team and
everyone is on one accord there is nothing they can't do. You see it in
families that are in agreement with each other, their family is blessed
for generations. When you have a team at your work place that just
seem to always out shine the others, it's usually because they agree with
each other and have confidence in each other to get the job done. When
you have a prayer partner it is a wonderful thing, to come together for
one common purpose. You bring your energy and they bring theirs,
it brings God on the scene double time. It's a dynamic, energizing
experience to pray together and see your prayers come to pass! Your
prayers of agreement are powerful beyond measure because you not
only open doors here on earth but you also open up the windows of
heaven to pure down blessings.*

You are blessed to be a Blessing!

*My prayer for you today is that whatever you
agree in prayer for will come to pass!*

Your scripture for today:

Mark 11:24

**Therefore I tell you, whatever you ask for in prayer,
believe that you have received it, and it will be yours.**

Observation:

*What is your belief system? For some it's 'I'll believe it when I see it!'
But if you already see it when does having faith come in to it? God
wants you to imagine holding whatever you've asked for in your hands
right now. That's why it says believe you have received it, which is
past tense. When you have already received something your attitude
is more confident about it, and you don't have to keep asking for it
because you already have it. The key is to hold on to that vision until
it is actually in your hands. Don't let one ounce of doubt enter into
that vision and you will see it come to pass!*

You are blessed to be a Blessing!

*My prayer for you today is that you will have big faith
to believe that your prayers are already answered!*

Your scripture for today:

John 5:19

Jesus gave them this answer: I tell you the truth, the Son can do nothing by himself; he can do only what he sees his Father doing, because whatever the Father does the Son also does.

Observation:

Little children will mimic their parent's actions and even what they say, good or bad! Parents are the earthly example they have to pattern themselves after until they get in the teenage years and decide they want to do their own thing. However, when you know at a young age that you have a powerful heavenly Father that has called you to greatness it can help you understand how wonderful you really are. You are in the family and that means that you can do what you have seen your Father do. That is amazing and puts you in a powerful place. You can do all things because you are in the family. Get your confidence level up; expect the best because it's your birthright.

You are blessed to be a Blessing!

My prayer for you today is that you understand how blessed you are because you have a powerful heavenly Father!

January 13

Your scripture for today:

John 10:14

**I am the good shepherd; I know my
sheep and my sheep know me.**

Observation:

*When sheep are out in the pasture there are times that some may
wander off from the rest of the flock. It's the shepherd's job to make
sure they get back in with the flock and to keep them out of danger.
They know the shepherds call and obey his leading. It's the same with
us being the sheep in God's pasture. You must be able to listen and hear
the voice of your good shepherd. There are many voices that want to
speak into your life. Many that feel they should tell you what is best
for you. But you must find time to be alone and listen for God's voice,
because he knows what is best for you. When God speaks into your
situation, believe it, do it and don't ask questions.*

You are blessed to be a Blessing!

> *My prayer for you today is that you will clearly hear the
> voice of the Good Shepherd leading and guiding your life!*

Your scripture for today:

John 16:13

But when he, the Spirit of truth, comes, he will guide you into all truth. He will not speak on his own; he will speak only what he hears, and he will tell you what is yet to come.

Observation:

Don't be like the newscasters who only bring the stories filled with drama, negativity and sensationalism. Because when you speak you are predicting your future. God sent the Spirit to you to be a guide but you have a lot to do with that. The Spirit cannot guide you in a different direction then what you say out of your mouth. He does not speak on his own; he only speaks what he hears you say or does what you tell him to do. If you speak about negative things, lack, doubt, down yourself, you are telling the Spirit what to produce in your life. So, speak words of hope, faith, love, peace, and abundance at all times and the Spirit will go to work to produce those things in your life.

You are blessed to be a Blessing!

My prayer for you today is that you will speak positive affirmations over your life so that your future will be bright!

Your scripture for today:

Acts 16:25-26

About midnight Paul and Silas were praying and singing hymns to God, and the other prisoners were listening to them. Suddenly there was such a violent earthquake that the foundations of the prison were shaken. At once all the prison doors flew open and every body's chains came loose.

Observation:

This is a perfect example of how God en habits the praises of his people. He loves to hear our praise as we worship him in spirit and with our voice. When we come together in praise and worship magnifying His holy name there is so much power that even those just listening will become free of their chains as well. Never underestimate the power we have when we praise God in music and in songs. When you are in that mode you are free from worry, anxiety and stress. You have opened your heart to receive and let your guard down. He will make everything right and suddenly in the midnight hour God will turn it around and work it out in your favor!

You are blessed to be a Blessing!

My prayer for you today is that you praise God today with all your heart and soul! Forget about your trouble and sing songs of praise!

Your scripture for today:

Deuteronomy 8:17-18

You may say to yourself, "My power and the strength of my hands have produced this wealth for me". But remember the Lord your God, for it is he who gives you the ability to produce wealth, and so confirms his covenant, which he swore to your forefathers, as it is today.

Observation:

God has blessed you to be prosperous in this life and to live a life of abundance. He has given you everything you need to be successful. All he wants is to be remembered for what he has given you and that is the ability to get that success. It's the same way when you give someone something that helps them achieve what they were going for and they never acknowledge that you had anything to do with it, you really don't like it. How about when someone takes an idea you gave them and act like it was their idea all along. Well we do that with God. Give honor to which honor is due and always give God the glory!

You are blessed to be a Blessing!

> *My prayer for you today is that you will remember that God has given you the power to create wealth. Acknowledge and always give him the glory!*

January 17

Your scripture for today:

Psalm 84:11

**For the Lord God is a sun and shield; the Lord
bestows favor and honor; no good thing does he
withhold from those whose walk is blameless.**

Observation:

*During the winter months there can be day after day of gloomy weather
and overcast skies. But when you get that one day of sunshine, it's so
refreshing and lifts your spirits for the day. It even causes you to forget
about those gloomy days and you are ready to go outside and breathe
again!*

*God will brighten your day and guard you from harm. He is the one
who lifts you up and causes others to want to do good things for you.
He is always ready to bless you and give you what you want as soon as
you ask for it. Just walk in his ways and praise his name. Thank God
for bringing the sun into our lives!*

You are blessed to be a Blessing!

*My prayer for you today is that God shines his rays of
sunshine, favor and blessing into your life today!*

Your scripture for today:

Psalm 23:4 amplified

Yes, though I walk through the (deep, sunless) valley of the shadow of death, I will fear or dread no evil, for you are with me. Your rod (to protect) and your staff (to guide), they comfort me.

Observation:

Believe that as you walk through the valley of your own situation, things are getting brighter and brighter with every step you take. It's not time to camp out and wallow in your sorrows, keep going! You are not trapped in it just look to God for the answer, He is right there with you and knows the best way out! Trust that God is right there leading your steps and guiding you in the right direction. When you see that light at the end of the tunnel run don't walk because you have made it!

You are blessed to be a Blessing!

My prayer for you today is that you will always remember that God is with you in the valley and on the mountain top!

January 19

Your scripture for today:

Proverbs 22:17-19

Pay attention and listen to the sayings of the wise; apply your heart to what I teach, for it is pleasing when you keep them in your heart and have all of them ready on your lips. So that your trust may be in the Lord.

Observation:

Sometimes the hardest things for us to do are pay attention and listen. So how can you apply your heart to what is taught if you are so preoccupied with the next thing and not present in the moment? We have become so used to getting things quickly we don't have time to listen to wisdom. However, there are options available that can be used to get the wisdom and insight we need. You can use your smart phone, listen to sirrus XM, or pop in a motivational cd in the car. Find the way that helps you to store up the wisdom you need in your hearts which will eventually be what you begin to speak. Take some time today to pay attention and listen to what God has to say!

You are blessed to be a Blessing!

My prayer for you today is that you will find the time to listen to wisdom. It can help you live your best life!

January 20

Your scripture for today:

Proverbs 24:3-4

**By wisdom a house is built, and through understanding
it is established; through knowledge its rooms
are filled with rare and beautiful treasures.**

Observation:

*No builder builds a house without first having a strong foundation.
Then the walls are constructed and the roof is placed. Therefore, when
you take the time to ask God for wisdom you also must ask for wisdoms
two friends; understanding and knowledge! With the 3 working
together in your life there is nothing you can't do. God's wisdom builds
you up on the inside, understanding his word establishes you and gives
a strong foundation, then knowledge lavishes you with blessings until
they overflow onto others.*

You are blessed to be a Blessing!

*My prayer for you today is that you have a sure foundation
of wisdom, understanding and knowledge of God!*

January 21

Your scripture for today:

Ecclesiastes 5:18-20

Then I realized that it is good and proper for a man to eat and drink, and to find satisfaction in his toilsome labor under the sun during the few days of life God has given him for this is his lot. Moreover, when God gives any man wealth and possessions, and enables him to enjoy them, to accept his lot and be happy in his work~ this is a gift of God. He seldom reflects on the days of his life, because God keeps him occupied with gladness of heart.

Observation:

God has given you a job to sustain you and if you are blessed enough you will be doing something you love! Just make sure you understand that God is your source. He is the one that is giving you all that you need to succeed and be happy in this life! He wants more than anything that you would prosper and be healthy, and that you continue to grow in your knowledge of who God is to you! Therefore, enjoy what you do every day, having wealth and enjoying all the things you have. You need to receive this gift from God and decide to be happy and not worrying about the day. Choose to have gladness of heart and reflect on the goodness of God every day!

You are blessed to be a Blessing!

My prayer for you today is that you will live a happy and fulfilled life, giving God all the glory!

January 22

Your scripture for today:

Ecclesiastes 7:11-12

Wisdom, like an inheritance, is a good thing and benefits those who see the sun. Wisdom is a shelter as money is a shelter, but the advantage of knowledge is this: that wisdom preserves the life of the possessor.

Observation:

Seeking the wisdom of God and obtaining it adds years to our life and money in our pockets. Have you ever heard the saying, "You pay for whatever you don't know"? Just knowing the right place to get our cars fixed can save money. Knowing the right directions can save gas, and knowing to ask God for wisdom in every situation will preserve our life and give us abundant blessings. But just like an inheritance you might not know who it will come from. Sometimes you can have a complete stranger give you a word of knowledge that will be a confirmation of something God already told you. Or you can be seeking the right way to go and someone will give you a word of wisdom that will get you to your destination faster. Wisdom is not determined by how old a person may be. Wisdom is from God and can even come through a child because they are a willing vessel and God knows how and when to get what he wants to get to you! Just be open to receiving God's wisdom!

You are blessed to be a Blessing!

My prayer for you today is that you will receive all the wisdom God has for you so that you will be blessed in every area of your life!

Your scripture for today:

Isaiah 46:11

I say: My purpose will stand, and I will do all that I please. From the east I summon a bird of prey; from a far-off land, a man to fulfill my purpose. What I have said, that will I bring about; what I have planned, that will I do.

Observation:

Can you see the integrity that God has? If we are going to be like God our word should be our bond! If we take the stand that "What I have said, that will I do, what I have planned, that will I do!" Think about how different things would be in the world if we all practiced this. Remember we should think before we speak, and do what we say we are going to do, when we said we are going to do it.

Is what you say a reflection of your purpose in life? What we speak about we bring about! If you are talking about things that have nothing to do with your goals in life then why are you talking about it? Sometimes we can get caught up in conversations that have no meaning, direction, or purpose. It's just mindless chatter that has no benefit. Be about the business of speaking positive ideas and brainstorming about future endeavors that will promote your purpose, vision and goals. You will be giving God something to work with and blessings will flow!

You are blessed to be a Blessing!

My prayer for you today is that you will speak about positive ideas that lead you to your God given purpose in this life!

Your scripture for today:

Matthew 10:19-20

But when they deliver you up, do not worry about how or what you should speak. For it will be given to you in that hour what you should speak; for it is not you who speak, but the Spirit of your Father who speaks in you.

Observation:

I have heard that one of people's biggest fears is speaking in front of other people. In high school speech class was a required subject that should be taken in your freshman year but the class was an elective and was always filled with seniors. That class was the last thing anyone wanted to take. Then there are those job interviews where you hope to say the right thing to get you that position that you desire.

Well, if you have ever been in a situation of wondering what to say, this is a clear promise to you that God will speak through you if you ask him to. If you ask God to use you as a vessel to say what he wants you to say he will, and it will be more powerful than you ever thought it could be. There is so much in you that God wants to bring out, but you have to be willing and allow God to use you! Just declare today that you will speak what God wants you to speak.

You are blessed to be a Blessing!

My prayer for you today is that you will not let fear overtake you when you have to speak but that you will let God speak through you!

Your scripture for today:

Ezekiel 36:26-27

I will give you a new heart and put a new spirit in you; I will remove from you your heart of stone and give you a heart of flesh. And I will put my Spirit in you and move you to follow my decrees and be careful to keep my laws.

Observation:

Who doesn't like new stuff? Don't you love it when you go to the store and buy something new? I call it shopping therapy! Or how about when you buy new groceries and you throw out the old things in the refrigerator to put in the new! Or what about when you get a new car! It smells awesome and even though you never saw that car on the highway before, now your awareness is awakened to see it everywhere! You get excited and thankful for the new things in your life.

Oh but we must thank God for a new Spirit and a new heart! He wants us to be renewed in our Spirit, soul, body, and our mind! Out with the old and in with the new you! God is making us new from the inside out. What a blessing it is to have a God who cares and wants us to be the best. You will have a new way of seeing things, a new outlook on life, a new purpose and new love for others. No matter what age, you can be made new!

You are blessed to be a Blessing!

My prayer for you today is that the new you will shine for all to see today!

January 26

Your scripture for today:

Jeremiah 1:5

Before I formed you in the womb I knew you, before you were born I set you apart; I appointed you as a prophet to the nations.

Observation:

If I say that I know you it's because we have had some kind of relationship. We have communicated together and I know you by name. If I see you from across the room I can call you and you will respond because I know you and you know me. Those that we allow to have a place in our lives are usually appointed by us to have that place. Otherwise they are just acquaintances that you are familiar with but you really don't know them.

Since God declares that he knew us before we got here, wouldn't that also mean that we knew him? Have you ever noticed how spiritually connected little children are with God? It's because they were hanging out with the Father before they were even formed in their mother's womb. Then as the child gets older, and been on earth for a while, they get further away from their Spiritual selves and forget that God created them and knew and appointed a path they should take. Just remember we can always stop, regroup and get back on track. Just ask God to give you the wisdom and direction and he will because he has already appointed you for greatness!

You are blessed to be a Blessing!

*My prayer for you today is that you will remember
the appointment that God predestined you for.
He knows your beginning from your end!*

28

January 27

Your scripture for today:

Matthew 12:33

Make a tree good and its fruit will be good, or make a tree bad and its fruit will be bad, for a tree is recognized by its fruit.

Observation:

Think of the tree in this scripture as our thoughts or attitude, and understand that they both bear fruit. But before there is a tree there must be a seed. The seed produces after its own kind. If you want apple tree you plant apple seeds, if you want a lemon tree you plant lemon seeds. Therefore, if you are planting seeds of negativity in your thoughts and watering them with bitterness, lack and doubt that is exactly what you will see growing in your life. In the same way planting seeds of positivity and watering them with joy, peace, love and forgiveness you will see so many blessing produced in your life! Be determined to produce good fruit in your life and it will show up in the lives of those around you and will continue to grow from generation to generation.

You are blessed to be a Blessing!

My prayer for you today is that you produce only good fruit in your life and the lives of your loved ones!

Your scripture for today:

John 14:27

**Peace I leave with you; my peace I give you. I do
not give to you as the world gives. Do not let your
hearts be troubled and do not be afraid.**

Observation:

*God's kind of peace is wonderful. You can rest in it, you can trust it,
and you will long for it. When your entire insides are turning and you
don't know which way to go. Stop and ask God for Peace. When you
are worried and it seems like your life is a ball of confusion, stop and
ask God for peace. Just like he got up in the midst of the storm and
said peace be still and the winds listened to him so will your situation.
Just ask for Peace!*

You are blessed to be a Blessing!

My prayer for you today is for peace in every area of your life!

January 29

Your scripture for today:

Romans 8:16-17

The Spirit himself testifies with our spirit that we are God's children. Now if we are children, then we are heirs-heirs of God and co-heirs with Christ.

Observation:

What if you were given a billion dollars today? What would you do? What would you think about? Where would you live? What kind of car would you drive? I am sure the sky would be the limit. Well you are rich, wealthy, and blessed beyond measure because you are an heir and a kingdom child. God wants you to know that you are blessed and that He wants to spoil you with all good things that this life has to offer. But not only that you have been blessed with eternal life that you can't even imagine! Accept His blessings by thinking, walking and talking like a child of a King!

You are blessed to be a Blessing!

My prayer for you today is that you know your inheritance is abundance, peace, joy and eternal life!

January 30

Your scripture for today:

1 Corinthians 2:9-10

However, as it is written: No eye has seen, nor ear has heard, no mind has conceived what God has prepared for those who love him but God has revealed it to us by his Spirit. The Spirit searches all things, even the deep things of God.

Observation:

God made you and knows exactly what you can handle. He has so many wonderful things prepared for you but he can only give it to you in bite sized pieces. He knows that if he gives you too much at one time it will blow your mind! But as you grow in the Lord and your Spirit grows to know Him he is then able to reveal more to you.

You must be ready to receive the goodness of God. Sometimes it comes in ways that you have not even thought of. God has prepared a life full of riches for those who love him. Take the time to be alone with God and allow him to reveal it through your Spirit. He has equipped you with everything you need and will guide you to everything you desire through your Spirit.

You are blessed to be a Blessing!

My prayer for you today is that you will grow in your Spirit to be able to receive all the blessings that God has in store for you!

January 31

Your scripture for today:

1 Corinthians 4:20

For the kingdom of God is not a matter of talk but of power.

Observation:

In the preliminary promotions for big boxing matches you will find the contestants talking about how they are going to defeat their opponent. They are usually talking big and bad to put fear in their opposition.

How many times have you heard someone talking loud but are not able to back up what they are claiming? The point is can you back up what you say with action that demonstrates the power backing your words? You are in God's kingdom therefore let your life be an example of His power that is at work in your life. God's word is powerful! You won't have to say a word for others to see it working in your life!

You are blessed to be a Blessing!

My prayer for you today is that the word of God
is working in powerful ways in your life!

FEBRUARY

Your scripture for today:

1 Corinthians 10:13

No temptation has seized you except what is common to man. And God is faithful; he will not let you be tempted beyond what you can bear. But when you are tempted, he will also provide a way out so that you can stand up under it.

Observation:

In every trial there are usually 6 elements present.

1. *Testing – an attempt to find out what you know.*
2. *Refining – to bring out any imperfections.*
3. *Interruption – to cause you to break any uniformity.*
4. *Audition – an opportunity to present your skills.*
5. *Life lesson – something for you to learn from.*
6. *Summons – a call for you to do something.*

When temptations and trials come you tend to think you are the only one experiencing it. You then isolate yourself and feel alone. But God is saying that whatever it is, it is common to man. There are others who have experienced it as well. But you can handle it, because God is with you as you go through it, and has already given you a way to get out of it. Just remember the 6 elements in your trial and know that you will come out of it better than ever!

You are blessed to be a Blessing!

> *My prayer for you today is that you find the treasure in your trial and know that God is blessing you through it!*

February 2

Your scripture for today:

2 Corinthians 1:3-4

Praise be to the God and Father of our Lord Jesus Christ, the Father of compassion and the God of all comfort, who comforts us in all our troubles, so that we can comfort those in any trouble with the comfort we ourselves have received from God.

Observation:

There are some who feel that as children of God that we shouldn't experience any kind of trouble in our lives. That it should always be smooth sailing. But that is far from true. God knows that we have an enemy who came to kill, steal and destroy. But God is always there to see us through any trouble we may face.

Therefore, when you have experienced trouble in your life and have felt the comfort from God, you can really relate to someone else that is having that same trouble. We are here to be the arms of God. Sometimes, all that is needed is a hug. Whatever it is, from listening to just spending time you will know what to do to comfort another as God has comforted you in the past.

You are blessed to be a Blessing!

> *My prayer for you today is that you will be the arms to comfort those who are experiencing trouble in their lives!*

February 3

Your scripture for today:

James 1:17

Every good and perfect gift is from above, coming down from the Father of the heavenly lights, who does not change like shifting shadows.

Observation:

Don't you love to receive a gift that you can tell some thought went into it? You know the giver of the gift thought about what you might like, what you need and what would bring a smile to your face! Well God knows exactly what you need and he has put much thought into the gifts he wants to give you!

There is no need to question whether God has good things for you. He states it over and over in the word. Every good gift is given to you by Him and he does not change like the weather. When He gives it, it's yours to keep! The way to keep it is by taking care of the gifts He gives you, use them for the good of the kingdom, and have a grateful heart.

You are blessed to be a Blessing!

My prayer for you today is that you receive every good gift that God has for you!

Your scripture for today:

James 1:12

Blessed is the man who perseveres under trial, because when he has stood the test, he will receive the crown of life that God has promised to those who love him.

Observation:

Do you remember being in school the teacher would give you a quiz? Sometime you would know ahead of time that they were coming and you would be able to study for them. But other times they would be pop quizzes, where the teacher would surprise the class with it to test you on what you should already know. Well life is like that, sometimes you know what's coming and other times you don't. But God is with you to help you persevere through test and trials and you will get the victory every time!

You are blessed to be a Blessing!

My prayer for you today is that you pass every test so that it becomes your testimony!

February 5

Your scripture for today:

Romans 8:31

**If God is for us, who can be against us? Who
can be our foe, if God is on our side?**

Observation:

*Sometimes it seems that the world is against you. It can be from family,
to friends, to co-workers, or bosses. But one thing that is for sure is
that you and God are a majority. The enemy will come to make you
think that you can't do anything right. But you don't have to take that
thought. Because, as long as God is on your side you have the power to
conquer anything that comes your way! When rejection comes, give the
hurt to God. When the bills can't get paid, give your concern to God.
When it seems that all your hope is gone and everyone is against you,
concentrate on pleasing God and he will give you favor with the people.*

You are blessed to be a Blessing!

*My prayer for you today is that you know that with God you
are able to conquer anything that comes against you!*

February 6

Your scripture for today:

Luke 8:50

Hearing this, Jesus said to Jairus, "Don't be afraid; just believe, and she will be healed."

Observation:

Have you noticed that many times before the miracle, God would send an angel or make sure to say "don't be afraid"? He knows that we get fearful when something supernatural is about to occur. But his comfort to us is to; just Believe! We don't have to be in control of everything. Let it go, and let God do it for you. Don't listen to the naysayers around you. Clear your space of any negativity. Believe in the impossible! Your dream may be bigger than your environment, so go for it, be not afraid; just Believe!

You are blessed to be a Blessing!

My prayer for you today is that you believe beyond your situation and have faith to move forward to your dreams!

February 7

Your scripture for today:

Luke 11:33

No one lights a lamp and puts it in a place where it will be hidden, or under a bowl. Instead he puts it on its stand, so that those who come in may see the light.

Observation:

You have the light of God in you. Be confident that it is shining for others to see. Let your light shine in this world and realize that with every step you take your path is lighting up. Your energy is magnetic, attracting others to you wherever you go so that you can bless them. Be confident in the God that is in you. He is the light that is shining bright through you! You may not see it, but others can. When you walk in a room your light goes before you. For some it will be comfort and the will gravitate to you. But for others it will be too bright because they want to stay in darkness. Just know that it's God who is causing your light to shine so be determined to let it shine, let it shine, let it shine!

You are blessed to be a Blessing!

My prayer for you today is that you will let your light shine for all to see!

February 8

Your scripture for today:

John 4:22-23

Yet a time is coming and has now come when the true worshipers will worship the Father in spirit and truth, for they are the kind of worshipers the Father seeks. God is spirit and his worshipers must worship in spirit and in truth.

Observation:

God's Spirit resides on the inside of you, so as you worship the Father you are connecting your Spirit with the Father and becoming one with God. When you worship Him in spirit and in truth for all that he has done and is doing in your life then praise Him for what is yet to come, you are blessing God. That is our way of giving back to Him by showing and telling Him how much we appreciate Him totally! Keep praising and worshipping the Father. Be faithful and true and His blessings will over flow in your life!

You are blessed to be a Blessing!

My prayer for you today is that you will understand how God loves it when you worship Him with all your heart and spirit. Not out of need but just because you know that He loves you!

February 9

Your scripture for today:

John 6:63

The Spirit gives life; the flesh counts for nothing. The words I have spoken to you are spirit and they are life.

Observation:

Because our spirit lives in a physical earth suit it's easy to forget that we are spiritual beings. We do everything we can to continue to look good on the outside. We read fitness magazines and look for ways to get healthy. We get nice designer clothes to dress up our earth suit. We dye it, color it, tan it and even get nips and tucks to keep it looking young. But what are we doing to feed our Spirit?

It is good to feed your spirit even more often than you feed your physical body. Of course you feed them in different ways. In the physical you eat food, and the spirit is fed by reading the word, walking in faith, meditating, and listening to motivational CD's. Sometimes your spiritual self is suffering from malnutrition; it hasn't been fed in quite some time! Start today to make a conscious effort to build up your spiritual body which can really give you abundant life!

You are blessed to be a Blessing!

My prayer for you today is that you do something
to build your Spirit every day!

February 10

Your scripture for today:

Romans 8:28

We know that in all things God works for the good of those who love him, who have been called according to his purpose.

Observation:

Have you ever been called on to do a job at work? Or maybe you have been asked to head up a project at Church. You might not have any idea how to accomplish the task but you were called on to do it! Well God has called you according to His purpose and he has already worked out the details because you love Him!

Isn't it good to know that God is working all things out for you! No matter what it looks like on the surface, he is working it out behind the scenes. He is doing things to help you whether you see it or not. He is blessing you right now; he has called you to fulfill his purpose on earth that only you can fulfill. Be encouraged that no matter what's going on he will make it alright but you have to be strong!

You are blessed to be a Blessing!

My prayer for you today is that you see pass the physical realm and know that God has already worked things out for your good!

February 11

Your scripture for today:

1 Corinthians 2:12

We have not received the spirit of the world but the Spirit who is from God, that we may understand what God has freely given us.

Observation:

Have you ever been in a situation where everyone around you were speaking another language? You may feel lost because you have no clue what they are saying. For all you know they could be making a joke or talking about you! On the other hand they could have been giving you the best compliment, but without knowing their language you are not able to receive it or thank them for it. Well that's how it is for those who have not accepted God. They cannot understand the things of our Father. They are foolish to them. But God has given us His Spirit to be able to discern the things he has for us. Give thanks to God for his Spirit that is living within us and the wisdom that he gives to all His children!

You are blessed to be a Blessing!

My prayer for you today is that you continue to understand the things of our Father!

Your scripture for today:

1 Corinthians 3:16-17

**Don't you know that you yourselves are God's
temple and that God's Spirit lives in you? If anyone
destroys God's temple, God will destroy him; for
God's temple is sacred, and you are that temple.**

Observation:

*When we go to church we are always so respectful of the sanctuary.
We even teach the kids to sit up, listen, and be on their best behavior.
You even make sure you look good when you go in your Sunday best.
However, the word says you are the temple! So every day you should do
the things that you do on Sunday, act the way that you act, and look
good because you are the temple that God's Spirit resides in. Sunday
should be a celebration of what was done all week and a time that all
God's temples come together for fellowship.*

You are blessed to be a Blessing!

*My prayer for you today is that you are an awesome
temple of God and reflect it every day!*

February 13

Your scripture for today:

Galatians 6:4-5

**Each one should test his own actions. Then he can take
pride in himself, without comparing himself to somebody
else, for each one should carry his own load.**

Observation:

*It's good to be independent and to work to get things that you desire.
Just remember that in all that you do make sure to stay dependent
on God to lead and guide you every step of the way. Be confident in
your ability and don't compare yourself to others because what God
has put you here to do cannot be compared to what he has placed in
someone else. There is a reason that you look the way you look, talk
the way you talk, was raise in the country or family you were raised
in and have the gifts and talents that you have! Don't underestimate
your abilities or question your past. It happened to grow you and to
promote you to the next level. Look to develop yourself into what God
has for you and when you do you will not have time to look and see
what others are doing!*

You are blessed to be a Blessing!

> *My prayer for you today is that you stay in your
> own lane and run your race with God!*

Your scripture for today:

Psalm 81:10

I am the Lord your God, who brought you up out of Egypt. Open wide your mouth and I will fill it.

Observation:

God saw his people suffering, enslaved, mistreated, and in bondage in Egypt; he knew he had to do something to free them. That is also why God has brought you all out of unpleasant situations and circumstances. Whatever your Egypt was, he has brought you out of it time and time again. God wants you to understand that He is still that God that will take care of you; He wants you to listen to His words and allow Him to fill your mouth with what to say. He is also the God that fills you to overflow with love, peace and financial blessings. Just remember he is the one that brought you out of Egypt. Thank God!

You are blessed to be a Blessing!

My prayer for you today is that you will remember that God loves you and is always here to help in your time of need!

Your scripture for today:

John 14:27

**Peace I leave with you; my own peace I
now give and bequeath to you.**

Observation:

*When you give someone something of yours to use or have it's a big
deal. You expect them to handle it with care and respect. Well God has
given us his own peace which has to be the best peace ever! Can you
imagine the kind of peace GOD must have! He made everything and
knows the beginning from the end. That is peace that's hard for us to
comprehend! It must be like knowing the outcome of a movie that you
are starting to watch. It might have some twist and turns but since
you know how it ends you can have peace. Therefore, God's peace is
available to use 24/7. It is your inheritance. He has given you power
and peace which are both wonderful gifts. Don't waste time whining,
crying, or throwing a fit when problems come. Instead, calm down and
think about the peace of God that is yours to keep.*

You are blessed to be a Blessing!

*My prayer for you today is that you accept
God's peace into your life today!*

Your scripture for today:

Isaiah 35:3-4

Strengthen the feeble hands, steady the knees that give way; say to those with fearful hearts, "Be strong, do not fear; your God will come, he will come with vengeance; with divine retribution he will come to save you."

Observation:

There are times when we feel weak because life is trying to beat us down. It might even look like there is no way out. You feel like you are in a maze of destruction with more trouble around every turn. But God will bring divine retribution and will save you!

Retribution is repayment of rewards, and God will bring divine repayment. That is why we have to be strong and have courage through the tough times. Remember that God's will for you is to prosper and be in health even as your soul prospers. Believe that God will restore everything you have loss. Just keep the faith, be strong and believe!

You are blessed to be a Blessing!

> *My prayer for you today is that you will be made strong when you are weak!*

February 17

Your scripture for today:

Isaiah 54:17

**"No weapon forged against you will prevail, and you
will refute every tongue that accuses you. This is
the heritage of the servants of the Lord, and this is
their vindication from me," declares the Lord.**

Observation:

*As children of God there will be various weapons that will try to form
against us. Untrue words spoken, false accusations, and even those
who become envious of your blessings. One of the enemies favorite
weapons that he loves to use against us is discouragement. He knows
when you get discouraged and loss hope he can get in and get you off
track. He forms that weapon in relationships, business endeavors,
school, and trying to find employment. Maybe you have been trying to
find that special someone and you have been getting turned down or
the ones you find are all jerks. You can get discouraged that there aren't
any good single people out there anymore and you want to give up and
quit. But how do you know if the next person you meet just might be
the right one for you? That is why I love this declaration, weapons may
form but they will not prosper. You can have confidence that God's got
your back and you are more than a conqueror and not a victim. Keep
going and remember that the enemy fights you the hardest when you
are close to getting the thing that God has for you. So be encouraged!*

You are blessed to be a Blessing!

*My prayer for you today is that you keep moving
forward no matter what it looks like!*

February 18

Your scripture for today:

Psalm 41:1

**Blessed is he who has regard for the weak; the
Lord delivers him in times of trouble.**

Observation:

*When you see someone that is financially weak and you bless them,
that's regarding the weak!*

*When you see someone that is emotional weak and you comfort them
that's regarding the weak!*

*When you see someone who is spiritually weak and you give them hope
that's regarding the weak!*

*When you help others who are in need God turns around and helps
you. You may think no one notices the good things you are doing, but
it is not going un-noticed! We are extensions of God hands here on
earth. As you are led by the Spirit of God to do things to help those in
need you are allowing God to use you as a vessel. Just remember the
more you give, the more you receive.*

You are blessed to be a Blessing!

*My prayer for you today is that when you see someone in
need that you are a vessel that God can use to help them!*

Your scripture for today:

Psalm 55:9-11

**Then my enemies will turn back when I call for help.
By this I will know that God is for me. In God, whose
word I praise, in the Lord, whose word I praise~ in God
I trust; I will not be afraid. What can man do to me?**

Observation:

*You have a God that is so in love with you that there is nothing that He
wouldn't do for you! He is ready to help you get through anything you
may be going through. Trust that God is here to back you up. He wants
you to call on him in your time of need. You don't have to struggle and
tackle things alone. You have God almighty to protect you, so what can
man do to you?*

You are blessed to be a Blessing!

*My prayer for you today is that you call on God
anytime and anyplace! He is here for you!*

February 20

Your scripture for today:

Hebrews 6:12

We do not want you to become lazy, but to imitate those who through faith and patience inherit what has been promised.

Observation:

We have so many examples of those in the Bible who persevered, kept the faith and were successful in what God had for them to do! In most of the examples they had major adversaries, obstacles and situations to get pass.

Don't give up or become lazy with what God has for you to do. Be patient it is coming to pass. Don't stop believing because God is working things out for your good. Make sure to speak positive words as you wait for your promise. Feed your mind by reading uplifting books. Meditate on the good things that God has already done for you and your wait will be sweet!

You are blessed to be a Blessing!

My prayer for you today is that you keep it moving and not become lazy about your dreams and goals!

February 21

Your scripture for today:

James 3:9

With the tongue we praise our Lord and Father, and with it we curse men, who have been made in God's likeness. Out of the same mouth come praise and cursing. My brothers this should not be. Can both fresh water and salt water flow from the same spring? My brothers, can a fig tree bear olives, or a grapevine bear figs? Neither can a salt spring produce fresh water.

Observation:

When I was a kid I used to hear people say, 'sticks and stones may break my bones but words will never hurt me.' Well that is so far from the truth that God says in the word!

Watch what you say and understand that you have a powerful weapon; your tongue! Death and life are in the power of the tongue. Choose to bless others with your words. Choose to encourage with your words. Choose to spread the good news with your words. Choose life you have the power in your words!

You are blessed to be a Blessing!

> *My Prayer for you today is that you use your words*
> *to bless and encourage others and yourself!*

Your scripture for today:

1 Peter 1:13

Therefore, prepare your minds for action; be self-controlled; set your hope fully on the grace to be given you when Jesus Christ is revealed.

Observation:

How do you prepare your mind for action? By reading the word, meditating daily, walking in faith and believing. Make sure and keep hope in your life. You can't have faith without first having hoped. Faith is the substance of things hoped for and the evidence of things not seen. You must keep hope alive in your life! You might look like the underdog in the fight but when your God shows up you are powerful beyond measure! Have confidence in your God and know that he has given you his powerful grace!

You are blessed to be a Blessing!

My prayer for you today is that you stay prepared to finish the work that God has for you!

February 23

Your scripture for today:

Psalm 34:12-14

Whoever of you loves life and desires to see many good days, keep your tongue from evil and your lips from speaking lies. Turn from evil and do good; seek peace and pursue it.

Observation:

With long life God will satisfy you. Have you ever known someone who told lies? Or have you known someone who always had excuses for why they didn't keep their word? They don't even realize that telling the truth would even sound better and that their excuses turn out to be lies after you have heard them over and over again. It just takes a made up mind to change and decide to tell the truth and not lie. To be a person of integrity and do what you say you were going to do when you said you would do it. When you seek peace and not drama, when you speak the truth and love one another, when we desire to do good things for others, you not only extend your life but also leave a legacy that will live on.

You are blessed to be a Blessing!

My prayer for you today is that you live a long life of integrity, truth, peace and love.

February 24

Your scripture for today:

Psalm 67:1-2

**May God be gracious to us and bless us and make
his face shine upon us, that your ways may be known
on earth, your salvation among all nations.**

Observation:

*I believe that God's ways are made known on the earth through us.
His salvation is spread as we talk about the good news of the gospel
and by our examples. We are role models whether we want to be or
not. Someone is watching you to see God's grace and blessings in your
life. There are many people who have separated from going to church
because they may have been hurt by negative, judgmental people who
look down on others. It's sad to think that a soul could be lost because
someone thinks you should look a certain way to attend church. Jesus
was judged by the religious leaders in His day and thought to be unfit.
But God is a God for all people. There is no one that walks this earth
who is perfect. Therefore the church is made up of imperfect people
striving to do the right thing and get filled up with God. Make sure you
are being the example of the grace that God has given you to others!
God's face is shining on you!*

You are blessed to be a Blessing!

*My prayer for you today is that Gods' grace and peace flows
over you from the top of your head to the soles of your feet!*

February 25

Your scripture for today:

Psalm 77:9-12

Has God forgotten to be merciful? Has he in anger withheld his compassion? Then I thought, "To this I will appeal: the years of the right hand of the Most High." I will remember the deeds of the Lord; yes, I will remember your miracles of long ago. I will meditate on all your works and consider all your mighty deeds.

Observation:

You may experience times when it feels like God is not with you and you begin to question his presence in your life. It is usually when you are in a test or trial. But you must remember that when a teacher is administering a test, the teacher is always quiet! They are giving you the opportunity to see what you already have in you. In school nobody enjoyed test day. There are so many things you have to remember and if you are not a good test taker you might freeze up under the pressure. You might have reviewed all your notes and could answer every question in your study time. But now the heat is on and you try to bring back to your remembrance everything that you know that you know. This is when you need to take a minute and breathe. Meditate on the goodness of God and how He is still here willing to perform miracles in your life. Just meditate on what he has done, because he will do it again. You will pass your test with flying colors when you make sure to put God in it!

You are blessed to be a Blessing!

*My prayer for you today is that you experience
the presence of God at all times!*

Your scripture for today:

1 Corinthians 14:13

God is not the author of confusion, but of peace.

Observation:

Always keep in mind that where there is confusion God is not in it. But He will bring you peace. So when you are feeling confused and it's hard to focus on anything but what is currently going on. You find yourself reacting to things instead of being pro-active about it. Your mind is going in all different directions. Your thoughts are here there and everywhere. It's like running in a maze, you get to a wall and turn around only to find another wall. Imagine coming to a crossroad and not knowing which direction you should go. How do you get yourself and your thoughts back into focus? How do you get out of this confusion? I believe that when you stop and ask God for peace in this situation, he will speak to you with a still small voice to help you out of the confusion. You must find a way to get still in your mind. Stop running yourself crazy and listen for Gods instruction and direction. The key is to stop and ask for peace. Don't hesitate to stop, ask, and listen!

You are blessed to be a Blessing!

> *My prayer for you today is that you will find*
> *peace in the midst of any confusion.*

February 27

Your scripture for today:

Psalm 45:7

You love righteousness and hate wickedness therefore God, your God, has set you above your companions by anointing you with the oil of joy.

Observation:

Do you know why you are set above your companions? They may wonder why you seem to get the good breaks and favor. Others may wonder why your energy is always positive or why you are able to lift others spirits. You love to see others succeed and be victorious in their lives. You just have that special something that everyone wants. The amazing thing about God is that it is for everyone who loves righteousness! Can you imagine God pouring oil all over you flowing from the top of your head to the soles of your feet? Being drenched with the oil of joy that comes from the Father himself! Well, God has anointed you with joy to be able to laugh through the toughest times. You have to receive it and be happy. Your joy will set you apart from others because you understand that it is from God. Joy is in your heart, it's in your soul, and it's all over you. You are anointed to have joy, bring joy, so claim it!

You are blessed to be a Blessing!

My prayer for you today is that you are immersed and anointed by God with the oil of joy!

Your scripture for today:

Psalm 63:6-8

On my bed I remember you; I think of you through the watches of the night. Because you are my help, I sing in the shadow of your wings. My soul clings to you; your right hand upholds me.

Observation:

I was taught as a young child to say my prayers before I lay down for sleep. It's a good practice to acknowledge and thank God for getting you through the day and praying for Him to keep you through the night. There is nothing like feeling safe and secure under the shadow of God's wings. Just like you prepare yourself to get ready for the day; you should also prepare your mind for the night. I believe you set yourself up to have a peaceful night's sleep and your spirit will be at rest with the Father. Have you ever noticed how many great ideas come in the morning when you have had that kind of rest? God can minister to you through the watches of the night and commune with your spirit better than any other time because you are still. When you know that you have the help you need and that God is your refuge, your protection and your strength, you will find rest for your soul in God alone!

You are blessed to be a Blessing!

My prayer for you today is that you have peaceful rest tonight and every night!

MARCH

March 1

Your scripture for today:

Psalm 25:4-5

Show me your ways, O Lord, teach me your paths; guide me in your truth and teach me, for you are my God my Savior, and my hope is in you all day long.

Observation:

Have you have ever been on a guided tour? The tour guide gathers the tourist into the area where the tour is to begin and leads the group through the exhibition. The tour guide is the one with all the knowledge of the exhibits and exactly how to get you to the exit. The tour guide knows the best path to follow to build up to the finale of the tour. If you get off track you might miss the spectacular ending. But sometimes the tour can get boring and mundane. You want to get some excitement and adventure only to find out that the tour guide had the best route and was able to give great information as the tour progressed. In the same way, you must allow God to show you the path that he has put in place for you. He is the best tour guide you will ever have for your life! He knows your beginning from your end. He even is not surprised when you get off track because your think you need more excitement in your life. Just know that when you decide to get back to the path that he has for you, it's ok to stop and ask for directions! He is the one who put you here in the first place. Be open and willing to follow His path. You have a built in guidance system which is your spirit. Ask and you will receive the direction you need!

You are blessed to be a Blessing!

My prayer for you today is that you allow God to show you his ways and paths for your life!

March 2

Your scripture for today:

Psalm 91:9-12

If you make the Most High your dwelling~even the Lord, who is my refuge~then no harm will befall you, no disaster will come near your tent. For he will command his angels concerning you to guard you in all your ways; they will lift you up in their hands, so that you will not strike your foot against a stone.

Observation:

I am reminded of having little ones running around the house and making sure that anything that could potentially hurt them is put up away from their reach. I would also be so protective of them when they were starting to walk. I would be right behind them ready to pick them up if they fall. Well, God has given His angels charge over you. To watch over your every step! He is concerned about every part of you and wants to make sure you are protected. He wants you to be safe and secure in your home, your car, your job, on the highways and byways. Where-ever you may go and whatever you may do God has provided protection for you! What a wonderful vow of protection. God has you covered when you make him your refuge. Trusting in his word, walking in the path he has for you and being obedient to his call. You have so many promises you can lean on. You are safe in his arms!

You are blessed to be a Blessing!

My prayer for you today is that you realize that God is protecting you so thank Him every day for your protection!

March 3

Your scripture for today:

Psalm 122:7-9

May there be peace within your walls and security within your citadels. For the sake of my brothers and friends, I will say, "peace be within you." For the sake of the house of the Lord our God. I will seek your prosperity.

Observation:

There are some people who thrive on drama. They look for it because they think that without a little drama in their life it's boring! So when there is no drama or confusion they create it. Sometime it's subconsciously done and they wonder why this is happening to them. Conduct a checkup from the inside out and make sure you are not a drama seeker! Are you allowing other drama seekers in your life? You have heard the saying birds of a feather flock together? Don't be surprised that when you decide to crave and demand peace, security, and prosperity in your homes, with your friends, family, and in your city, those drama seekers will stop coming around. When you begin to recognize that peace is your inheritance. You will begin to live your best life now! God wants you to have peace within because that is where He dwells!

You are blessed to be a Blessing!

My prayer for you today is that you have
peace in every area of your life!

March 4

Your scripture for today:

Psalm 145:3-4

Great is the Lord and most worthy of praise; his greatness no one can fathom. One generation will commend your work to another; they will tell of your mighty acts.

Observation:

One day my daughter and I were listening to music and an old song came on that I didn't think she would know because it was out before she was born. However, she had a little bit of a twist on it. So I asked how you know this song. She stated that this was some new artists' song and that the version we were listening to they were singing it wrong! This made me think about how we must pass it on. All the great and wonderful things God has done for you. You must pass it on to the next generation. His word has lived for thousands of years and it is up to you to continue to spread the good news by just sharing what he has done for you individually. There are those who will come to use the word of God and give it a new twist to appeal to a new generation. But we must make sure that the basic foundation of truth is kept intact. I was happy to know that that old song was still being played and the main foundation of the song was still there. So make sure you are telling about God's greatness every day so that it will live on from generation to generation!

You are blessed to be a Blessing!

My prayer for your today is that you pass on all the miracles and greatness that God has shown you to the next generation!

March 5

Your scripture for today:

Jeremiah 31:13

**...I will turn their mourning into gladness; I will
give them comfort and joy instead of sorrow.**

Observation:

*I am so thankful to God for the times that I had loved ones go on to
be with the Lord that my mourning was not as it would be if I had no
hope! When you know that your loved one is with God they are not lost
because you know where they are. Although you may miss them you
can be at peace because you know you will see them again!*

*God has promised to be with you always and to never leave or forsake
you. Especially in your time of mourning and sorrow he will be there
to comfort your soul and give you his peace. Just ask him to reveal his
precious presence to you. Also ask for the right friends who will be real
friends that God himself would have chosen for you. He will comfort
you and cause you to rejoice. So get ready for the joy!*

You are blessed to be a Blessing!

> *My prayer for you today is that you may mourn
> but you will have comfort and peace from your
> heavenly Father and your joy will be renewed!*

March 6

Your scripture for today:

Matthew 14:28-31

Lord. If it's you, Peter replied, "Tell me to come to you on the water". "Come", He said. Then Peter got down out of the boat, walked on the water and came toward Jesus. But when he saw the wind, he was afraid and, beginning to sink, cried out, "Lord, save me!" Immediately Jesus reached out his hand and caught him. "You of little faith," he said. "Why did you doubt?"

Observation:

Have you ever been summons by Jesus to do something that seemed to be too difficult or outrageous? How many times do you pray to God for a miracle and when you get it you begin to look around at the wind, listen to people, become afraid of the success and begin to sink. God has already given you the power to be successful in this life. But there may be times when He calls on you to step out of your comfort zone and move to another area, or start a new business, or talk to someone who intimidates you. You will be able to succeed as long as you don't look at the circumstances or begin to analyze why this could not happen. I have to give it to Peter because he got out of the boat!!! He allowed fear to set in and began to sink but he got out of the boat and knew who to call on for assistance. Just remember to call out for God's help before you are sunk. God will bring you out, he just wants you to have faith. Stop looking around and keep the focus on Him.

You are blessed to be a Blessing!

My prayer for your today is that you have the courage to get out of your comfort zone when God calls you to come out!

March 7

Your scripture for today:

Matthew 16:19

I will give you the keys of the kingdom of heaven; whatever you bind on earth will be bound in heaven, and whatever you loose on earth will be loosed in heaven.

Observation:

When you give someone a key to your home it's because you trust them with your prized possession. Maybe you are going on a vacation and you leave your keys with the neighbor or friend to watch over things while you are away. You have faith that your home will be in the same condition if not better than you left it. They water your plants, and feed the pets. You know they will handle whatever needs to be done or you would not have given them your keys! Well, God has given you the keys to the kingdom of heaven. He trusts you to take care of the power that he has given you. God has given you the power to create your situations, circumstances and outcomes for your life. When you pray, your prayers are so powerful that you can change things in heaven and on earth. You have the power to shut things down and to open up the windows of heaven to pour out blessings in your life. God gave you the keys and the power is within you!

You are blessed to be a Blessing!

> *My prayer for you today is that you use the keys to the kingdom of heaven to make your life the best it can be!*

Your scripture for today:

Mark 12:30

Love the Lord your God with all your heart and with all your soul and with all your mind and with all your strength.

Observation:

Have you experienced the different stages of love? There is the infatuation stage when you can't see anything wrong with the person you have feelings for. They can't do any wrong in your eyes. I remember being in this stage and couldn't eat and my Dad would say, you better eat because you can't live on love alone. But, I really think he knew this was that first stage of puppy love and that it would change. The funny thing is that it usually did change when the next stage is entered which is the awakening stage. You wake up to the little things your partner does that get on your nerves. If you get pass this stage and are still together you are usually on your way to staying in that relationship. Love is that powerful emotion of your heart that when you love with all your might it is the most amazing experience ever! That is how your love for God should be. Think loving thoughts and have images of love in your mind all day about God. Make every effort to stay in the final stage of Love with your heavenly Father! Because God is Love!

You are blessed to be a Blessing!

My prayer for you today is that you live, move and walk in love for your father God all day and every day!

March 9

Your scripture for today:

Proverbs 24:3-4

**By wisdom a house is built, and through understanding
it is established; through knowledge its rooms
are filled with rare and beautiful treasures.**

Observation:

*I have been in the Real Estate business in one form or another by
selling homes, buying homes and relocating families from place to
place. I have watched homes being built from the ground up and I
am always amazed by the expertise of the builders and workers. They
were given a blueprint of the home by the Architect and with their
wisdom, knowledge and understanding they are able to build a house
and that to me is amazing! You have dreams and goals that you want
to see manifest in your life. With God's wisdom, understanding and
knowledge your dreams will be established. He is the architect of your
dream. He is the one who placed it there in the first place. This means
you must go to God to receive the wisdom to make your dream or goal
come to pass. You will be given the creative ideas and all the knowledge
you need to succeed. He will lead you to be in the right place at the
right time and meet the right people to accomplish greater things than
you could ever imagine!*

You are blessed to be a Blessing!

*My prayer for you today is that you go to the Architect of your
dreams to get wisdom, knowledge and understanding!*

March 10

Your scripture for today:

1 Peter 1:13

Therefore, prepare your minds for action, be self-controlled, set your hope fully on the grace to be given you when Jesus Christ is revealed.

Observation:

Have you ever planned an event like a baby shower, super bowl party, wedding or any festive event? There is so much preparation that goes into it days, weeks and sometimes months ahead of time. You have to coordinate many different vendors and services. From decorations to food, the preparation ahead of time will determine if the event is done with excellence or not! Preparing your mind is an everyday thing; it's not a one-time process. You can make up your minds to have a great day before you get out of bed every morning. Positive self-talk is the best thing in preparing your mind. Speak positive affirmations about yourself every morning. Believe and be confident about it and watch how you can create a wonderful day. This is the day the Lord has made be glad and rejoice in it!

You are blessed to be a Blessing!

My prayer for you today is that you prepare your mind to be ready for Jesus on a daily basis!

March 11

Your scripture for today:

Galatians 6:9

**Let us not be weary in well doing, for in due
season we shall reap, if we faint not.**

Observation:

*Have you ever been so exhausted that you just can't make it another
step? You have given all the energy you have and just don't think you
can make it any further. Sometimes problems seem so overwhelming
that the road ahead seems too steep to climb. You go through times
when you want to give up. But you have to remember that even though
continuing to move forward seems painful, it is far better than giving
up. If you keep going God will give you that second wind and you
will be infused with supernatural power that only God can give. God
is doing a good work in you! You are about to get your harvest of
blessings. He can and will do more for you and through you as long as
you don't grow weary and faint!*

You are blessed to be a Blessing!

*My prayer for you today is that you will get your
second wind from almighty God and reap the
harvest of blessings he has in store for you!*

Your scripture for today:

Psalm 1: 1-3

Blessed is the man who does not walk in the counsel of the wicked or stand in the way of sinners or sit in the seat of mockers. But his delight is in the law of the Lord, and on his law he meditates day and night. He is like a tree planted by streams of water, which yields its fruit in season and whose leaf does not wither. Whatever he does prospers.

Observation:

I have noticed that any advice you need is available to you through the internet. You can research illnesses, gardening, repairs, services and many more. They usually have reviews from others who have used them or have comments about the situation. Just remember that you have the guidance you need in any situation. It is always available to you. Why do you go to others for advice when your Creator is here to direct your paths? If you want to know the purpose of your life and how your experiences fit into that purpose, ask your Creator. God is available, accessible and waiting to counsel you! He is the one that will make everything prosper for you! So seek Him first and you will yield much fruit!

You are blessed to be a Blessing!

*My prayer for you today is that you seek
God first for advice and direction!*

March 13

Your scripture for today:

Psalm 52:8

But I am like an olive tree flourishing in the house of God; I trust in God's unfailing love forever and ever.

Observation:

Greece is full of olive tree orchards and they call the Olive Tree, "the tree that feeds the children". God wants you to flourish in all that you do so that you can be the one able to give in any situation. Like an olive tree that feeds the children, God will build you up so that your branches reach high and wide to others. In addition, the olive tree produces olive oil which is used for food but also used as an oil to anoint. You are anointed, fruitful, and blessed because you trust in God's unfailing love!

You are blessed to be a Blessing!

My prayer for you today is that you will be anointed, fruitful and blessed by God today!

Your scripture for today:

Psalm 5:11-12

But let all who take refuge in you be glad; let them ever sing for joy. Spread your protection over them that those who love your name may rejoice in you. For surely, O Lord, you bless the righteous; you surround them with your favor as with a shield.

Observation:

When Hurricane Ike rolled through Texas I had never experienced anything like it before. All the neighbors got together and helped each other board up the houses because the news was letting us know when it was scheduled to hit our area. We were given enough warning a head of time to stay in the area or evacuate. So we chose to take refuge in our home. Well it turned out that this storm was bigger than the Meteorologist expected and there was much damage done to property. Our roof caved in and major work had to be done but God was with us the entire time because he is the best refuge in any storm you can face in life! As children of God we have his protection and you must realize how much He loves you. Believe that God is on your side. Material things can be replaced. Our home was repaired and to an even better state than it was before, because He surrounds us with his favor, grace and mercy! Be glad that you have a God that provides and shelters us in the times of storms!

You are blessed to be a Blessing!

*My prayer for you today is that you can rejoice
in the shelter of almighty God!*

March 15

Your scripture for today:

Romans 8:28

And we know that in all things God works for the good of those who love him, who have been called according to his purpose.

Observation:

Crossword puzzles are great to stimulate the mind. You can get them in various levels of difficulty, different designs, images and pieces count. One day I was working on a puzzle and I thought for sure they must have left some pieces out. I couldn't seem to get it to work out the way the picture was showing on the box. However, somehow as I continued to work it, the pieces seem to fall into place and I was able to finish it. This reminded me of how there are times when our lives are a puzzle to us. We can't figure out how things are going to work out. But when you put your trust in God who created you, everything will work out for your good! Be encouraged no matter what's going on, he will make it alright. He knows every piece in the puzzle of your life! God is working behind the scenes working on your behalf even when you can't see it! Trust and believe that it will all work out for your good and you will be the perfect picture that God created you to be!

You are blessed to be a Blessing!

> *My prayer for you today is that you understand*
> *that God created you and called you so no matter*
> *what it looks like He will fix it for your good!*

March 16

Your scripture for today:

Psalm 46:1

God is our refuge and strength, an ever-present help in trouble.

Observation:

Did you know that others can see and are aware of those who will get things done? If you are that person, I am sure you have been asked to be on committee after committee. When you are, you can get in over your head with all the obligations and things you have committed to do, than you try to cope with feeling overwhelmed in order to get everything done. Just put your hands up and scream at the top of your lungs H—E—L—P! Share your load with the perfecting presence of God and your burden will become easier and the load will be lighter. He will give you creative ideas to work through the situation with ease and grace. He is your help in whatever trouble you find yourself in.

You are blessed to be a Blessing!

My prayer for you today is that you remember to ask God for help with anything in your life because he cares about it all!

March 17

Your scripture for today:

Acts 2:28

**You have made known to me the paths of life;
you will fill me with joy in your presence!**

Observation:

Years ago when you wanted to take trip and drive from your location to your vacation destination you would get a map or atlas and figure out the best route to get you there. Or you could contact a company and get it done for you with books of every State you will go through which is still available for you to do. However, these days just about every car has a navigation system in it or people use their smart phones to guide them to their destination. But when it comes to guidance and direction for your life who do you go to? God wants you to seek him to discover what path you should take. Instead of going to other people go to your creator and ask for direction. You know that he has already gone before you making your crooked places straight and he is just waiting for you to stop and ask for help! His way is the way to joy, peace and happiness!

You are blessed to be a Blessing!

*My prayer for you today is that you will look
to God to lead and direct your path!*

Your scripture for today:

2 Corinthians 4:17-18

For our light and momentary troubles are achieving for us an eternal glory that far outweighs them all. So we fix our eyes not on what is seen, but on what is unseen, for what is seen is temporary, but what is unseen is eternal.

Observation:

In the sport of boxing there are about 18 weight classifications. There is lightweight, featherweight, heavyweight, and super heavyweight just to name a few. You wouldn't see a match where a lightweight boxer was boxing a heavyweight boxer. That would be an unfair match! Well God is the Super Heavyweight and our lightweight troubles are no match to what our God can do. Be encouraged that no matter what is going on there is a light at the end of the tunnel. There is calm on the other side of the storm. Realize that these things did not come to stay, they came to pass. You are on the right path or the obstacles would not come, see pass it and know that God will fight your battle and you win every time!

You are blessed to be a Blessing!

My prayer for you today is that you can be sure that you are a winner because God's won every fight!

March 19

Your scripture for today:

Proverbs 15:13

**A happy heart makes the face cheerful;
but heartache crushes the spirit.**

Observation:

When you are happy everything seems to be better in your life! You can choose to be happy every day of your life. There was a song when I was young with a catchy Reggae beat called 'Don't worry be happy'. We all need to concentrate on being happy more. Happiness comes from within; it's making a decision not to sweat the small stuff. Situations and circumstances will come to steal the joy that you have within. Just remember that Jesus came to give you abundant life. He has already walked out your footsteps. He knew before the beginning of time what you would be facing this very moment so laugh more and remind yourself that God has it all under control!

You are blessed to be a Blessing!

*My prayer for you today is that you will be
happy every day in every way!*

Your scripture for today:

Isaiah 35:3-4

Strengthen the feeble hands, steady the knees that give way; say to those with fearful hearts, "Be strong, do not fear; your God will come. He will come with vengeance; with divine retribution he will come to save you."

Observation:

We are all ministers that can speak encouraging words to those who are in fear. When you know that God will fight their battles for them you can bring them strength and comfort. The enemy may be feeling really great right now, even gloating over what seems to be a victory. But when you have done all to you can to stand, stand anyway. Just be reminded that God has divine retribution or payback for you! Keep your faith and don't give in because vengeance is the Lord's and you are on the winning side!

You are blessed to be a Blessing!

My prayer for you today is that you will be strong and have no fear because God is with you!

March 21

Your scripture for today:

Romans 8:15-16

**Because those who are led by the Spirit of God are sons
of God. For you did not receive a spirit that makes you a
slave again to fear, but you received the Spirit of sonship.
And by him we cry *Abba* Father. The Spirit himself
testifies with our spirit that we are God's children.**

Observation:

*My children have certain privileges in my house that others do not
have. They can walk in un-announced, go in the refrigerator, and
raid the pantry and even camp out on the sofa. Because they are my
children they can ask for things that others can't ask me for and I am
ready to give it to them. Of course I want to make sure it's for their good
and will not harm them. If they call me I make myself available for
them. If they need advice I ask God to give me the wisdom to give them
what they need. Well your Father is always there, leading, guiding,
protecting, and providing for you. Spend some time with him getting
to know him better. You can ask him to help you understand yourself,
your life and the role he plays in them both. You can ask him to teach
you to forgive and to love. There are so many things you can go to your
Father God for, but it requires spending some time with him on a daily
basis. He loves you with an everlasting love.*

You are blessed to be a Blessing!

*My prayer for you today is that you have a close
relationship with your heavenly Father!*

March 22

Your scripture for today:

Romans 8:18

I consider that our present sufferings are not worth comparing with the glory that will be revealed in us.

Observation:

Understand that all the trials, problems, difficult situations, and unpleasant circumstances you encounter are all preparation for promotion. They will make you stronger, they will increase your faith, they will bring you out and you will be a totally different person. Just keep moving toward God in the midst of the trials. Keep confessing the word and communicating with your Father. The glory will be revealed in you! So remember weeping may endure for a night but JOY comes in the morning!

You are blessed to be a Blessing!

> *My prayer for you today is that you will increase your faith as God take you to your next level!*

March 23

Your scripture for today:

Psalm 40:5

Many, O Lord my God, are the wonders you have done. The things you planned for us no one can recount to you; were I to speak and tell of them, they would be too many to declare.

Observation:

There are so many things that God has done for you whether you know it or not. He has so many wonderful blessing and so many open doors for you. Be willing to receive the blessings of the Lord and walk through those opened doors without fear! God has planned a wonderful life for you; don't block it by being closed minded to new things. The blessings he has for you don't always come in the form you thought it might come in. Stay open to his direction!

You are blessed to be a Blessing!

My prayer for you today is that you remind yourself of all the wonderful things that God has done for you!

March 24

Your scripture for today:

Proverbs 16:2-3

**All a man's ways seem innocent to him, but motives
are weighed by the Lord. Commit to the Lord
whatever you do, and your plans will succeed.**

Observation:

*What is the reason you do what you do? There are reasons you are
successful and there are reasons you are not. The only reason a person
doesn't have the life they want is because somewhere in the back of
their mind they don't believe they deserve it! Remember God knows
what you are thinking and the reason you do what you do! When you
commit your plans to God he is excited and ready to make the plans
successful! Commit your plan to Him and believe that it will come to
pass.*

You are blessed to be a Blessing!

*My prayer for you today is that you commit
everything you do to the Lord!*

March 25

Your scripture for today:

Jeremiah 1:5

Before I formed you in the womb I knew you, before you were born I set you apart; I appointed you as a prophet to the nations.

Observation:

Isn't it amazing to think that God knew you before you were even conceived in your mother's womb? Recognize that there is nothing you are going through that God didn't know was going to happen. Everything you experience is a part of your journey, but you were chosen and appointed to be great! Believe it, receive it, and declare it. You are a child of God and blessed beyond measure!

You are blessed to be a Blessing!

My prayer for you today is that you realize that you were conceived for greatness!

Your scripture for today:

1 Corinthians 2:9-10

However, as it is written: "No eye has seen, no ear has heard, no mind has conceived what God has prepared for those who love him~but God has revealed it to us by his Spirit.

Observation:

God loves you so much that he gave you his Spirit in order for you to have wisdom in all areas of your life. God has big plans for you to leave a legacy of spiritual wealth. Material wealth is wonderful but as you attain the prosperity you also have to remember to feed your Spirit. Prayer, fasting, and reading the word are great ways to feed your Spirit. Be devoted to living a spirit-filled, peace-filled life and leave a legacy that is more valuable than money!

You are blessed to be a Blessing!

My prayer for you today is that you remember to feed your spirit and leave a legacy of spirituality for your family!

March 27

Your scripture for today:

Psalm 77:11-14

**I will remember the deeds of the Lord; yes I will remember
your miracles of long ago. I will meditate on all your works
and consider all your mighty deeds. Your ways, O God, are
holy. What god is so great as our God? You are the God who
performs miracles; you display your power among the peoples.**

Observation:

*Thank God for all the miracles and deeds done every day in your
lives! Yes you can look back and see all the wonderful things God has
done but don't forget that he is doing them right now! You are reading
this message because you are blessed to have sight and you woke up
this morning! Meditate on His goodness, thank Him daily for always
being there for you and praise Him for the miracles he is performing
every day!*

You are blessed to be a Blessing!

*My prayer for you today is that you will meditate
on the goodness of God all day!*

Your scripture for today:

Hebrews 13:15-16

Through Jesus, therefore, let us continually offer to God a sacrifice of praise~the fruit of lips that confess his name. And do not forget to do good and to share with others, for with such sacrifices God is pleased.

Observation:

When you sacrifice it's because the circumstances are not favorable or the time isn't quite right. So when you give God a sacrifice of praise things may be going crazy around you and it might be easier to complain, but instead you begin to praise God for the good, in the midst of the trouble, that is a sacrifice and God is pleased!

You are blessed to be a Blessing!

My prayer for you today is that you give up a sacrifice of praise because God is good all the time!

March 29

Your scripture for today:

1 Peter 4:10-11

Each one should use whatever gift he has received to serve others, faithfully administering God's grace in its various forms. If anyone speaks, he should do it as one speaking the very words of God. If anyone serves, he should do it with the strength God provides, so that in all things God may be praised through Jesus Christ. To him be the glory and the power forever and ever. Amen.

Observation:

Have you ever noticed that when you give to others in need you get blessed? Giving is a way to serve and minister to Gods people. It doesn't have to be money. It can be giving your time to serve. It could be listening to someone who needs a friend. It could be speaking an encouraging word to lift someone's spirits. Whatever it is you have been given the grace to do it. Grace is undeserved favor or a gift. It is the undeserved forgiveness, kindness and mercy that God gives you. So remember that the gift God has given you has been assigned to you to fulfill God's purpose on earth. You are covered by God's grace! Use it to the fullest so others will be blessed and praise God because of you!

You are blessed to be a Blessing!

My prayer for you today is that you use the gifts God has given you to be of service to His people!

March 30

Your scripture for today:

1 Corinthians 10:23

**"Everything is permissible"~but not everything is beneficial.
"Everything is permissible"~but not everything is constructive.**

Observation:

Your creator has given you free will! You have the freedom to choose whatever you want to do in this life. The choice is yours! You can choose life or death, you can speak things into existence, and you can live a life of defeat or victory. Everything is permissible but is it beneficial or constructive? This is the believer's freedom. Let's choose to live a life of blessings and victory!

You are blessed to be a Blessing!

> *My prayer for you today is that you choose
> to speak life and victory every day!*

March 31

Your scripture for today:

Hebrews 10:23

Let us hold unswervingly to the hope we profess, for he who promised is faithful.

Observation:

If you have ever watched the trapeze artist in the Circus swing from rope to rope it's amazing and so exciting. They have the act where one person is swinging from his knees on the bar and another does a flip in the air toward him so he can catch him in mid-air. To the crowds amazement they do it without a problem. But they had to hold firmly to each other's hands and believe that it would work in order to make it happen. In the same manner you must hold firmly to what you believe and don't let doubt enter in. As you say with your mouth what you hope for or want, God is dispersing angels to make it happen. Keep saying what you want and believing it in your heart, than watch it manifest in your life!

You are blessed to be a Blessing!

My prayer for you today is that you hold firmly to profession of faith and believe that God will make it happen!

APRIL

April 1

Your scripture for today:

Psalm 16:7-8

I will praise the Lord, who counsels me; even at night my heart instructs me. I have set the Lord always before me. Because he is at my right hand, I will not be shaken.

Observation:

God is waiting to give you instruction, sometime the only time he can talk to you is while you sleep. He may have even awakened you at 3:00 in the morning to get your attention. It's not that you just can't sleep, maybe its God trying to tell you something! Be confident with the knowledge that God is concerned about you! He is interested in every aspect of your life. Don't be shaken by what things might look like. Our God is able to turn it around for your favor!

You are blessed to be a Blessing!

My prayer for you today is that you allow God to get your attention at all times!

April 2

Your scripture for today:

Isaiah 40:31

**Those who hope in the Lord will renew their strength.
They will soar on wings like eagles; they will run and
not grow weary, they will walk and not faint.**

Observation:

*I have heard the story of the eagle and how it can soar to heights higher
than any other bird. That's how the Lord wants to bring you up, allow
him to be your strength. He wants you to be strong and not weak. But
when you are weak he is strong. Rely on him, call on him, he will show
up for you. The eagle's wings are extremely wide and strong, able to
fly through the wind with ease and grace. Just know that the Lord will
carry you and keep you. He will renew your strength and you can
count on Him! As it says in Galatians 6:9 Let us not become weary in
doing good, for at the proper time we will reap a harvest if we do not
give up.*

You are blessed to be a Blessing!

*My prayer for you today is that you will allow the Lord to carry you
through anything you might be going through. He is your strength!*

April 3

Your scripture for today:

Galatians 5:14-15

The entire law is summed up in a single command: "Love your neighbor as yourself." If you keep on biting and devouring each other, watch out or you will be destroyed by each other.

Observation:

God has given you the ability and senses you need to Love. You also have the ability to hate. When you realize that everyone is made in the image of God, and that he is Love, it is obvious what you should be doing and how you should be treating your fellow man. Examine your heart and make sure you are walking in Love and not hate. When your neighbor, brother, sister, or whoever gets blessed don't hate, congratulate! You are a child of God so be Happy for them. God will reward you because your heart is right!

You are blessed to be a Blessing!

My prayer for you today is that you will be love in motion!
Showing love to all that come into your presence!

April 4

Your scripture for today:

2 Corinthians 10:7

You are looking only on the surface of things. If anyone is confident that he belongs to Christ, he should consider again that we belong to Christ just as much as he.

Observation:

When people or things come against you, remember to look deeper into the situation. There will be trials and Jesus even reminds us that they will come. But when you look at it with your Spiritual eyes you are able to see pass the circumstances. Be confident in the fact that you belong to Christ and he doesn't want you to be blinded by the situation. He has already walked out your footsteps and knows your desired result. He is working behind the scenes to bring it to you. Just keep believing.

You are blessed to be a Blessing!

My prayer for you today is that you will have spiritual eyesight and be able to discern the things of God!

April 5

Your scripture for today:

1 Peter 5:10-11

**And the God of all grace, who called you to his eternal
glory in Christ, after you have suffered a little while,
will himself restore you and make you strong, firm and
steadfast. To him be the power forever and ever. Amen.**

Observation:

*God is in the restoration business. He will give you strength when you
feel weak! He will make you firm not moved or shaken easily! He will
make you steadfast and established! Look for the victory because it is
surely coming. If you see yourself as the victim you will react in fear
and as long as you are in fear you are blocking your blessing. So be
strong in the Lord and the power of his might, because restoration has
already begun.*

You are blessed to be a Blessing!

*My prayer for you today is that you will be strong in the Lord and
the power of His might because you are victorious with Him!*

April 6

Your scripture for today:

Ephesians 3:19

May you experience the love of Christ, though it is too great to understand fully. Then you will be made complete with all the fullness of life and power that comes from God.

Observation:

Can you imagine being filled up with God's love? His love never changes; it remains constant and available in an unlimited supply. It is available to you just be open to receive it. Hold thoughts and images of love in your mind. When you can be filled with love, move in love and see love in all things, you are living the truth of your soul. This is being filled with God's love.

You are blessed to be a Blessing!

My prayer for you today is that you are filled to overflow with the love of God!

April 7

Your scripture for today:

Luke 16:10

Whoever can be trusted with very little can also be trusted with much, and whoever is dishonest with very little will also be dishonest with much.

Observation:

I can remember my first car. It left a lot to be desired. I was just excited to be able to get from point A to point B without having to walk or take public transportation. But I knew that if I took care of what I had that I would eventually get what I really wanted. God wants to give us everything we want but will give us as much as we can be trusted with. Be determined to understand the purpose for your desires and dreams. Then when we ask for more we will handle it better because we understand the reason God is blessing us with it. Show yourself and God that you can take care of what he has already given you by being a good steward over it, and have a grateful heart.

You are blessed to be a Blessing!

My prayer for you today is that you take care of what you have so that you can be blessed with what you really want!

April 8

Your scripture for today:

1 John 4:4

You, dear children, are from God and have overcome them, because the one who is in you is greater than the one who is in the world.

Observation:

I have my favorite radio station that I listen to every day. It's motivational, uplifting and inspirational. However, there are many other stations that are much different. Depending on what you choose to listen to there is a station for you and you can tune into that station. When you tune into God's frequency you will amaze yourself with what you can do. The Spirit of God is in us flowing through our bodies and giving us insight in all things. Similar to that radio station that inspires and motivates, the spirit of God is always here to uplift us from the inside out. You are an overcomer because God created you and gave you His Spirit to make sure of it! No matter what's happening in the world you are an overcomer!

You are blessed to be a Blessing!

> *My prayer for you today is that you tune into the Holy Spirit every day to get uplifted, motivated and inspired!*

April 9

Your scripture for today:

Proverbs 24:3-4

**By wisdom a house is built, and through understanding
it is established; through knowledge its rooms
are filled with rare and beautiful treasures.**

Observation:

*When you take the time to ask God for wisdom you also must ask
for wisdoms two friends; understanding and knowledge! With the
3 working together in your life there is nothing you can't do. God's
wisdom builds us up on the inside, understanding his word establishes
us and gives a strong foundation, then knowledge lavishes us with
blessings until they overflow onto others.*

You are blessed to be a Blessing!

*My prayer for you today is that you understand that
you can have the wisdom of God any time you ask!*

Your scripture for today:

Psalm 26:2-3

**Test me, O Lord, and try me, examine my heart
and my mind; for your love is ever before me,
and I walk continually in your truth.**

Observation:

God knows what is in our heart and what we are thinking about. It is a confident person who can boldly say to God test me! Having a pure heart and thinking good thoughts is what God wants for us. It says in Philippians 4:7-8

And the peace of God, which transcends all understanding, will guard your hearts and your minds in Christ Jesus. Finally, brother, whatever is true, whatever is noble, whatever is right, whatever is pure, whatever is lovely, whatever is admirable if anything is excellent or praiseworthy think about such things.

You are blessed to be a Blessing!

*My prayer for you today is that you have the
peace of God that no one can understand!*

April 11

Your scripture for today:

James 1:5-8

If any of you lacks wisdom, he should ask God, who gives generously to all without finding fault, and it will be given to him. But when he asks, he must believe and not doubt, because he who doubts is like a wave of the sea, blown and tossed by the wind. That man should not think he will receive anything from the Lord; he is a double-minded man, unstable in all he does.

Observation:

When you ask God for anything you must believe it is already done. I believe he dispatches his angels to do what we ask. Keep a vision of the end result in your mind, speak about it already happening. Take time in your day to meditate on the blessing that you will receive. But if you begin to doubt that it will be done God has to call the Angels back. It's like you are wishy-washy and you don't really know what you want. If you have ever met someone like that it's confusing. They want it, then they change their minds and don't want it. From God's perspective He will wait until you have a made up mind. Realize that you control it by what you think and say. Believe that you receive it when you pray for it! It is yours!

You are blessed to be a Blessing!

My prayer for you today is that you will have a made up mind so that you will get everything you ask God for!

April 12

Your scripture for today:

John 15:5

**I am the vine; you are the branches. If a man
remains in me and I in him, he will bear much
fruit; apart from me you can do nothing.**

Observation:

*Have you ever tried to do something in your own power and got
frustrated and confused? Stress comes when we continue to try to
figure things out instead of stopping to ask God for His guidance. I have
never seen a tree that can live without being connected to the roots.
You know that when the roots are healthy the tree will be strong and
bear much fruit. In the same manner, when we stay close to God, our
source, we are able to do powerful and amazing things. Sometimes we
amaze ourselves! But the key is to be led by the Spirit of God and you
can do all things and bear much fruit!*

You are blessed to be a Blessing!

*My prayer for you today is that you stay connected
to the vine and bear much fruit!*

April 13

Your scripture for today:

Psalm 62:7-8

I depend on God to save me and to honor me. He is my mighty rock. He is my place of safety. Trust in him at all times, you people. Tell him all of your troubles. God is our place of safety.

Observation:

You can depend on God to be there for you at all times. He is in you and wants you to believe, trust and have faith in Him to get you through every aspect of your life. As you learn to trust Him, you must also trust yourself. God does His work through you, and if you don't trust yourself to do what He has purposed you to do, then 'He is' limited by you. But God's purpose will prevail; He will move it to another willing vessel. So trust Him and trust yourself!

You are blessed to be a Blessing!

> *My prayer for you today is that you learn to depend on God for everything you need!*

April 14

Your scripture for today:

Psalm 138:7-8

Though I walk in the midst of trouble, you preserve my life; you stretch out your hand against the anger of my foes, with your right hand you save me. The Lord will fulfill his purpose, for me; your love, O Lord, endures forever do not abandon the works of your hands.

Observation:

You must have complete confidence in the Lord's protection over your life. He is walking with you in the midst of the fiery furnace. God will not leave you or forsake you. He is your rock and foundation. I have a couple of friends who have experienced sky diving. For some it's just another adventure but for others it's was a way to face their fear of heights. They all describe the sense of freedom they felt when they actually released everything and fell out of the plane. It was like floating in air! It was peaceful and just amazing! Well that's how it should be with God! In the midst of your trouble, know that you can lean on, stand on, and even free fall. He will be there to catch you. Have faith and confidence in his protective hands.

You are blessed to be a Blessing!

My prayer for you today is that you release everything to God and free fall into his protective arms!

April 15

Your scripture for today is:

John 10:14

**I am the good shepherd; I know my
sheep and my sheep know me.**

Observation:

*You must be able to listen and hear the voice of your good shepherd.
A good shepherd knows exactly how to keep his sheep. He knows their
every move and the ones that he may have to watch because they
want to go astray. There are many voices that want to speak into your
life. So many that feel they should tell you what is best for you. But
you must get by yourself and listen for God's voice, because he knows
what is best for you. When God, your good shepherd, speaks into your
situation it will be the best thing for you. Just believe it, do it and don't
ask questions.*

You are blessed to be a Blessing!

> *My prayer for you today is that you will listen to the voice
> of God at all times. He will lead you into your destiny!*

Your scripture for today:

Romans 15:4

**For whatever things were written before were written
for our learning, that we through the patience and
comfort of the Scriptures might have hope.**

Observation:

*Remember that the word was written for you to learn, to get wisdom,
and to understand how to live this life. Have you ever read a book
and allowed your imagination to run wild through the pages? There
are books that can motivate you to do more with your life, teach you
how to cook, and teach you to do just about anything. The Bible can
inspire you in every area of your life. Be encouraged by studying the
word daily. When you know what the word says you can apply it to
your life and have more hope for the future.*

You are blessed to be a Blessing!

*My prayer for you today is that you study the word
to learn what God has to say about your life!*

April 17

Your scripture for today:

2 Corinthians 12:9

**But he said to me, "My grace is sufficient for you,
for my power is made perfect in weakness."**

Observation:

*Have you ever just stopped in the middle of the madness and cried out
to God for help! He is right here waiting for your request. We try to do
everything in our own power and have supernatural power ready to
assist us. Surrender your will in the situation, count to three, and say
GOD I NEED YOUR HELP! His grace is sufficient at all times and in
every situation. When we are weak He is strong. Call on His power
and receive the grace of God!*

You are blessed to be a Blessing!

*My prayer for you today is that you receive the
grace of God every day in every way!*

April 18

Your scripture for today:

Proverbs 13:12

**Hope deferred makes the heart sick, but when
the desire is fulfilled, it is a tree of life.**

Observation:

*Hope is the key ingredient to have faith. Remember faith is the
evidence of things hoped for... There are many who become sick because
they have become discouraged. The main tool that the enemy uses is
discouragement. He knows that if he can get you to lose your hope and
become discouraged he can then move on to affect your heart. When
your heart is hurt it can lead to depression and all other dis-eases. But
God is always with you to give you hope that your future will be bright.
Don't give into the tools of the enemy and allow that discouragement
to enter in. Keep your hope and believe that God will do it! Continue
to hope for new things in your life. Dream bigger dreams! Allow your
imagination to reach new heights and trust that God will bring it to
pass.*

You are blessed to be a Blessing!

*My prayer for you today is that you keep dreaming big dreams
and hope for better things in your future and it will be so!*

April 19

Your scripture for today:

2 Thessalonians 2:16-17

May our Lord Jesus Christ himself and God our Father, who loved us and by his grace gave us eternal encouragement and good hope, encourage your hearts and strengthen you in every good deed and word.

Observation:

God's love and encouragement for you never dies, it lives on through setbacks, disappointments in life, and even when you are downing yourself. God's message is be encouraged and have good hope be strong in the Lord and the power of his might! The greater one lives within you so don't be moved by things that may be coming against you! You are a child of the highest God who has protected you before and will continue to do it! So be encouraged!

You are blessed to be a Blessing!

My prayer for you today is that you remember that God is for you, love you, and is your biggest fan!

April 20

Your scripture for today:

Proverbs 12:18

**Reckless words pierce like a sword, but the
tongue of the wise brings healing.**

Observation:

*Our words can edify, bless, encourage, heal, and comfort others. If we
decide to think before we speak it can make all the difference. On the
other hand our words can tear down, curse, wound and abuse others.
Our words are like seeds that are planted in ground of the mind and
heart of the one who is listening. When those seeds take root they can
grow to be words that will bless them or negative words that can haunt
them for all of their life. Think before you speak! Ask yourself will my
words heal or kill? Be the one who speaks healing and blessings to
everyone around you!*

You are blessed to be a Blessing!

*My prayer for you today is that you speak words of
healing and blessing today and every day!*

April 21

Your scripture for today:

2 Corinthians 9:12

This service that you perform is not only supplying the needs of God's people but is also overflowing in many expressions of thanks to God.

Observation:

Sometimes you don't always realize that what you do helps others to see God. Whatever service you are called to do it is important and supplies a need of God's people. You are anointed to do it and therefore will cause others to thank God for you! Every time you supply a need; God is hearing your name, when you perform a good deed; God is hearing your name. When you give of your time; God is hearing your name. God is hearing your name as those you help thank Him for you! God is in the blessing business and you are in line for His blessings to chase you down just continue to be a willing vessel and your blessings are always coming!

You are blessed to be a Blessing!

My prayer for you today is that you will seek to be a blessing to others, so that God can turn around and bless you abundantly!

Your scripture for today:

2 Corinthians 9:8

**And God is able to make all grace abound to you,
so that in all things at all times; having all that you
need, you will abound in every good work.**

Observation:

*Having children of my own I can relate to wanting to raise them to
be fully equipped with the knowledge they need to get ahead in life. I
knew that the more exposure I could give them would be good for them
to excel in every area of their lives. We are God's representatives on
earth, why shouldn't you have all that you need to get things done? All
you have to do is accept the fact that you are a child of the highest God
and there is nothing he will withhold from you that is good for you.
Being good parents we want the best for our children so why shouldn't
God provide all that you need to be successful in every area of your
life? His grace is available to you so be confident in your ability to get
the job done!*

You are blessed to be a Blessing!

*My prayer for you today is that you will believe
that you can do all things with God's grace!*

Your scripture for today:

James 1:12

Blessed is the man who preservers under trial, because when he has stood the test, he will receive the crown of life that God has promised to those who love him.

Observation:

Have you noticed that just before a blessing everything seems to get a little tougher? Many give up or quit before the blessing comes. They can misinterpret the difficulty of the situation thinking that it's not God's will for it to be done. But have you ever heard the saying, when the going gets tough the tough get going? Remember the test always comes before promotion. When you were in school there was a final exam to pass to the next grade. Well it is the same with life; the test comes to prepare you for your next level! You pray more when you're in a difficult situation! You learn more about yourself and what you are capable of handling! Be determined to pass the test and move on to what God has in store for you!

You are blessed to be a Blessing!

My prayer for you today is that you will press on in the difficult times to get your blessing!

April 24

Your scripture for today:

Psalm 62:11

One thing God has spoken, two things have I heard; that you, O God, are strong, and that you, O Lord, are loving. Surely you will reward each person according to what he has done.

Observation:

You serve a strong and loving God who wants you to be all, do all, and have it all! He is a rewarder of those who seek him, who do his word and love others. Continue to do his will and be responsive to the Spirit of God. He gives you instructions, if you are listening, that will guide you every day. Part of His favor and rewards are in the quiet nudges he gives you, be open and aware so that you will be blessed abundantly!

You are blessed to be a Blessing!

My prayer for you today is that you listen closely to the guidance the Holy Spirit is giving you!

April 25

Your scripture for today is:

Acts 16:25-26

About midnight Paul and Silas were praying and singing hymns to God, and the other prisoners were listening to them. Suddenly there was such a violent earthquake that the foundations of the prison were shaken. At once all the prison doors flew open and every body's chains came loose.

Observation:

This is a perfect example of how God en habits the praises of his people. He loves to hear your praise as you worship him in spirit and with your voice. When we come together in prayer there is so much power that even those just listening will become free of their chains as well. Never underestimate the power you have when you pray. He will make everything right and suddenly in the midnight hour God will turn it around and work it out in your favor!

You are blessed to be a Blessing!

My prayer for you today is that you lift your praise up to the Lord every day. When the praises go up the blessings come down!

April 26

Your scripture for today:

John 6:63

The Spirit gives life; the flesh counts for nothing. The words I have spoken to you are spirit and they are life.

Observation:

It is good to feed your spirit even more then you feed your physical body. Of course you feed them in different ways. The physical you eat food, and the spirit is fed by reading and understanding the word, walking in faith, meditating, praying, and listening to motivational CD's. Sometimes your spiritual self is suffering from malnutrition and crying out for food. Be sensitive to your spirit and start to build it up! Feed it every day and build it up so that you will be super sensitive to the voice of the Father! He will speak life into you and give you hope for the future!

You are blessed to be a Blessing!

> *My prayer for you today is that you will feed your spirit with everything that will build you up so that you will get supernatural insight into all things!*

April 27

Your scripture for today:

Psalm 89:15

**Blessed are those who have learned to acclaim you,
who walk in the light of your presence, O Lord.**

Observation:

*To acclaim your Lord is to declare Him ruler or winner by enthusiastic
approval. When you choose to put God first in your life and realize
that he is in everything you do you are acclaiming God. If you have
ever been to your favorite teams' game or watched them on television
you can get very excited and shout with enthusiasm when they score
or win the championship. You acclaim your team by wearing the
shirts, putting the flag on your car and announcing to everyone that
is your team! Just consider that without God's love, God's mercy and
grace, nothing you consider important would be possible. Acclaim Him
today; get excited because you are on the winning team!*

You are blessed to be a Blessing!

> *My prayer for you today is that you will get excited about
> the God we serve and acclaim his goodness every day!*

April 28

Your scripture for today:

Ephesians 6:19

**Pray also for me, that whenever I open my mouth,
words may be given me so that I will fearlessly
make known the mystery of the gospel.**

Observation:

Have you ever been around someone who loves to talk? They talk about any and everything whether they have knowledge of it or not. Sometimes you would like them to just be quiet and listen but that doesn't seem to be their way. It's like they're talking loud but saying nothing! Ask that the words of your mouth and the meditation of your heart will always be acceptable to God. When you ask God to put the words in your mouth every time you open it, you are truly being used as a vessel. Remember that you are a messenger of God. Don't be afraid to make that message known to others. Be bold, fearless, and a willing vessel.

You are blessed to be a Blessing!

My prayer for you today is that you seek to please God with you words and that they will be edifying to all those listening!

Your scripture for today:

Psalm 77:9-12

Has God forgotten to be merciful? Has he in anger withheld his compassion? Then I thought, "To this I will appeal: the years of the right hand of the Most High." I will remember the deeds of the Lord; yes, I will remember your miracles of long ago. I will meditate on all your works and consider all your mighty deeds.

Observation:

There are times that it feels like God is not with you and you begin to question his presence in your life. It is usually when you are in a test or trial. When you think about the story of Job and how blessed he was then everything was taken away from him. He never cursed God or lost his faith in the God that he served. Even though his friend were urging him to do so, he never considered it because he knew God would deliver him! When you are in those tough times, friends and family hate to see you suffer but God will see you through it if you keep your faith and get through that test. Not only will you be restored but you will receive double for your trouble! God is still performing miracles; just meditate on what he has done before, because he will do it again.

You are blessed to be a Blessing!

My prayer for you today is that you remember the miracles that God has performed in your life! Meditate on them and be encouraged!

April 30

Your scripture for today:

Jeremiah 6:16

**This is what the Lord says: "Stand at the crossroads and look;
ask for the ancient paths, ask where the good way is,
and walk in it, and you will find rest for your souls.
But you said, 'We will not walk in it.'**

Observation:

We have all had times when we were given great advice by a parent or someone older than us and we think they don't know what's happening now! Only to do what we wanted to do and discover that their advice was the right advice! When wisdom is speaking stop and listen! They have been there and done that or seen it happen in their lifetime and what the outcome was. Be open to sound Godly instruction so that you can live a life of peace!

You are blessed to be a Blessing!

*My prayer for you today is that you will follow
the path that the Lord has chosen for you!*

MAY

Your scripture for today:

2 Kings 6:16-17

**"'Don't be afraid,' the prophet answered. 'Those who are
with us are more than those who are with them.' And Elisha
prayed, 'O Lord, open his eyes so he may see.' Then the Lord
opened the servant's eyes, and he looked and saw the hills
full of horses and chariots of fire all around Elisha."**

Observation:

*Our false perception is the biggest cause of fear and frustration! If
you live without faith, your perception is restricted to what you see
with your eyes and hear with your ears. With this limited input, it's
easy to live in fear - and so many become frustrated and discouraged
with their day to day life. But as your faith and understanding of God
increase, you are able to trust in what you cannot physically see or
hear. You will be able to see with your spiritual eyes and visualize the
dream and desires that God placed in you. He will give you the step by
step plan to make it happen. Don't be afraid, just do it!*

You are blessed to be a Blessing!

*My prayer for you today is that your eyes will be opened
to all the good things that God has in store for you!*

Your scripture for today:

Psalm 27:13-14

I would have lost heart, unless I had believed that I would see the goodness of the Lord in the land of the living. Wait on the Lord; be of good courage, and He will strengthen your heart, wait, I say, on the Lord!

Observation:

You have to stay encouraged and not lose heart. The dreams and desires God has placed in you will come to past! Believe that God placed that dream in your heart therefore he will help you make it happen. We usually have a problem with the wait on the Lord part. We usually decide to help God out while we wait, just in case He needs our help to figure out how and when the dream needs to be completed. Remember God knows when you are ready to receive that blessing! His timing is always best. Trust and believe and you will have the goodness of the Lord in the land of the living!

You are blessed to be a Blessing!

My prayer for you today is that your every dream that God placed in your heart will come to past as you believe in his goodness!

May 3

Your scripture for today:

Proverbs 16:2-3

**All a man's ways seem innocent to him, but motives
are weighed by the Lord. Commit to the Lord
whatever you do, and your plans will succeed.**

Observation:

*I have seen many court situations where there is a Judge and jury. The
plaintiff and defendants Lawyers are there to plead the case for their
client in hopes of winning the case. No matter who is right or wrong
the case is presented based on the evidence that they have and how
well they can convince the jury that their client is innocent. There are
many cases where the facts can be twisted by getting the jury to see
them in a totally different way than they first perceived it. Since the
Judge and Jury are made up of people they can only go by the law of the
land and human emotion plays apart in the verdict as well. But God
knows what you are thinking and the reason you do what you do! God
sees the heart of man and knows exactly what went down and why you
do what you do! Keep your motives and your heart pure. When you
do for others, it doesn't matter if anyone else knows about it or not.
God's blessings and favor on your life will be apparent to others. He is
the ULTIMATE JUDGE and Jury! Plus you have the best Lawyer you
could ever have JESUS! Commit your plans to the Lord. Let Jesus plead
your case and you will have a victory every time!*

You are blessed to be a Blessing!

*My prayer for you today is that you keep your motives and
your heart pure and allow Jesus to plead your case for you!*

May 4

Your scripture for today:

Psalm 40:5

Many, O Lord my God, are the wonders you have done. The things you planned for us no one can recount to you; were I to speak and tell of them, they would be too many to declare.

Observation:

The first time I saw the Grand Canyon I was amazed at the sight. I literally cried the first time I saw the Statue of Liberty in New York. These are just a couple of examples of some of the wonders that are visible to us in the natural realm. God has performed so many wonderful things in my life that when I think about His goodness my soul is filled with joy! God has so many wonderful blessings in store for us that have not been done yet. When you contemplate what he has already done it will help you appreciate what is yet to come! He is opening doors of abundance, doors of opportunity, doors of new relationships, so many open doors. But, you have to be willing to receive the blessings of the Lord and walk through those opened doors without fear! God has planned a wonderful life for you; don't block it by being close minded to new things. The blessings he has for you don't always come in the form you thought it might come in. But if you stay open to receive you will experience the awesome wonders of God in your life. Stay open to his direction and step out in faith!

You are blessed to be a Blessing!

My prayer for you today is that you will walk through every open door that God puts in your path! Allow God to amaze you with his wonderful blessings!

May 5

Your scripture for today:

Romans 8:28

And we know that in all things God works for the good of those who love him, who have been called according to his purpose.

Observation:

I love to decorate and I recently took a trip out to Los Angeles to help my daughter decorate her new apartment. She wanted a desk to study at so we went to the furniture store and found the perfect desk that would fit the space in her apartment. However, when the sales person brought it out it had to be assembled. We thought ok how hard can it be? Well, through lots of prayer and persistence we finally got it put together. What I realized in the process is that the creator of the desk built it so that all the pieces worked together. If you put a piece in the wrong spot it would throw the entire project off. I even tried to pry a piece into what I thought was the right spot and it just was not working. So I took it out, followed the direction closely and it all worked out. God is our creator and even when you are going through tough times, he has and will work it out for your good. Remember God is not surprised by anything you might go through. He has already walked out your footsteps; he knows the obstacles you were going to face and every test that you were going to have to pass. They are designed to make you stronger and get you to another level if you trust him and ask him for direction. There is a lesson in it but He knows the purpose you are here for and He will not leave you because you have been called!

You are blessed to be a Blessing!

My prayer for you today is that everything works out in your favor because you are called according to His purpose.

Your scripture for today:

1 John 3:18

**Dear children, let us not love with words or
tongue but with actions and in truth.**

Observation:

*There are so many people who have pets. Whether it is a dog, cat, bird
or a combination of all, their pets are loved and are treated like family.
My Mom loved her miniature French Poodle named Sherry. She knew
Sherry so well and truly loved her. What's amazing to me is even
though the words may not have been spoken the actions of love and
care spoke louder! When we show our love through our actions, people
will know we are Christians by our love! You can talk about love all
day but are you showing your love through what you do and how you
treat others. Our actions speak louder than words! It's not about what
you say but what you do. Be an example of love through your actions,
give people your time, and give them a smile, sometimes all they need
is a hug! Be love in motion and what you give out you will get back!*

You are blessed to be a Blessing!

*My prayer for you today is that other's will know
you are Christian because of your love!*

May 7

Your scripture for today:

Micah 7:7

**I watch in hope for the Lord, I wait for God
my Savior; my God will hear me.**

Observation:

*Have you ever been first at the traffic light waiting for it to turn green
and before you can step on the gas the car behind you is honking
their horn because you didn't go fast enough? Have you been in the
drive through and ordered your food but it's taking longer than you
think it should take to get your fast food? How about when your
cellphone battery is out and you have to wait for it to get charged up
to use it again! Sometimes waiting can be the hardest thing in this
instant society. Our patience doesn't need to develop because we can
microwave food, call on cell phones, text message, use search engines
to find out anything we want to know including information about
people. God wants us to develop the fruit of the Spirit called patience.
Instead of running yourself crazy, stop and wait for God's direction.
Remember waiting is still an action. You can meditate, study the
Word, pray, listen to things that will feed your Spirit. Don't just sit
down, do the things God is directing you to do, just make sure you
seek him first. You will get so much done with less time because you
waited on God's guidance!*

You are blessed to be a Blessing!

*My prayer for you today is that you wait on the Lord
for His guidance in every area of your life!*

May 8

Your scripture for today:

Psalm 141:3

**Set a guard over my mouth, O Lord; keep
watch over the door of my lips.**

Observation:

*Be careful of the things you choose to talk about. The Israelites took
much longer to get to the promise land because they murmured and
complained about everything. At first they were amazed at the miracles
they were experiencing. Then after a while those miracles were not good
enough. They had been there, done that, and got the tee shirt. I have
learned that when you complain you remain but when you praise you
raise! If you watch the news it's always the negative viewpoint that
is shared, which can cause you to complain along with everyone else
about how things look in the natural! Remember your words create
your future. You can call those things that are not as though they were,
until they are. God's economy is doing great! Keep in mind that you are
in the world but not of the world. When we all begin to speak about
the positive things we want to see happen today, we will experience a
better tomorrow!*

You are blessed to be a Blessing!

*My prayer for you today is that you will raise up to new levels
because when the praises go up the blessings come down!*

May 9

Your scripture for today:

2 Corinthians 10:7

**You are looking only on the surface of things. If anyone
is confident that he belongs to Christ, he should consider
again that we belong to Christ just as much as he.**

Observation:

*When Jesus walked the earth he was criticized by religious leaders of
that time because of who he was around and how he dressed. They
couldn't figure out how he called himself the King of Kings and didn't
dress the part. They saw him as the carpenter's son and couldn't see
His greatness. We must be careful not to be quick to criticize the
outer appearance of others. They might be doing the best they can
with what they have. There are many people who turn away from
the Church because they are offended by judgmental people. But we
much consider that they belong to Christ just like everyone else who
confesses the Lord. See pass the surface and understand that we must
not judge a book by its cover or judge a person because of their outer
appearance. Look deeper and get to know that persons heart. You will
be pleasantly surprised that beyond the surface there is a loving, kind
and beautiful spirit!*

You are blessed to be a Blessing!

*My prayer for you today is that you are led by your spirit to look
beyond the surface and not judge anyone by their outer appearance!*

May 10

Your scripture for today:

Ecclesiastes 5:18-20

Then I realized that it is good and proper for a man to eat and drink, and to find satisfaction in his toilsome labor under the sun during the few days of life God has given him for this is his lot. Moreover, when God gives any man wealth and possessions, and enables him to enjoy them, to accept his lot and be happy in his work~ this is a gift of God. He seldom reflects on the days of his life, because God keeps him occupied with gladness of heart.

Observation:

One of things we must realize is that we were all born with a gift. Think about what you would do even if you didn't get paid. What would it be? It is awesome when you can work at what you're passionate about! What I have seen happen is that we fall into the normal way of life. You are taught to get a good job with benefits and be happy. Well, I believe that God created us individuals and gave us different gifts for a reason. Life is too short not to be happy about what we do every day. This is how God wants you to be! Enjoying what you do every day, having wealth and full of joy. You may be doing a job that you dislike right now, but begin to declare that you are happy no matter what the circumstances may be. Receive the gift of joy from God and decide to be happy and not worrying about the day. Make a choice to have gladness in your heart. When things get crazy just remind yourself that God gave you the gift of joy so don't give it away or allow someone or something to steal it!

You are blessed to be a Blessing!

My prayer for you today is that you will begin to be happy and full of joy, working in your passion and using the gifts that God placed in you!

May 11

Your scripture for today is:

Psalm 16:7-8

I will praise the Lord, who counsels me; even at night my heart instructs me. I have set the Lord always before me. Because he is at my right hand, I will not be shaken.

Observation:

With modern technology is has become increasingly harder to be present in the moment. People are always checking their smartphones to see the latest status from their friends, get the newest information on their favorite celebrity, and even stay connected to the news. However, God wants to give you his status but sometime the only time he can talk to us is while we sleep. He would love to speak to us all day if we allow him to. Have you ever stopped in the middle of the day and just acknowledged him? He may have been trying to get your attention. Put him first in everything you do, ask him for instruction and direction then take a minute to listen because God is trying to tell you something!

You are blessed to be a Blessing!

My prayer for you today is that you will take the time to get God's status. It just might be just what you needed to hear at that moment!

May 12

Your scripture for today:

Isaiah 40:31

**Those who hope in the Lord will renew their strength.
They will soar on wings like eagles; they will run and
not grow weary, they will walk and not faint.**

Observation:

Have you ever been tired of being tired? There are times when we just go, go, and go, doing everything for everybody. You have given until you can't give any more. This is the time when you are in need of the Lord's energy boost. Sounds like a drink you buy in the store like Red Bull! However, this is so much better because it renews you with the power of God. Stop for God's energy boost and allow him to be your strength. He wants you to be strong and not weak. As it says in Galatians 6:9 Let us not become weary in doing good, for at the proper time we will reap a harvest if we do not give up.

You are blessed to be a Blessing!

*My prayer for you today is that you will run and not grow
weary because you know God's right there with you!*

Your scripture for today:

Proverbs 10:22

**The blessings of the Lord brings wealth,
and he adds no trouble to it.**

Observation:

It's so encouraging to know that as God blesses us we will be wealthy in so many ways. Having joy, happiness, laughter, health, family, and friends is a part of having wealth. As we open our heart to receive the blessings, and mature in our ability to handle the wealth in our lives, God is able to give us more. If we can't handle a little wealth why would God give us more? Be faithful with the little and increase will come. Remember God says he wants us to prosper and be in health even as our soul prospers. So get ready to receive your blessings!

You are blessed to be a Blessing!

*My prayer for you today is that you have all
the wealth that the Lord has for you!*

May 14

Your scripture for today:

Lamentations 3:22-23

**It is of the Lord's mercies that we are not consumed,
because His compassions fail not. They are new
every morning: great is Thy faithfulness.**

Observation:

*Thank God for the new morning! With every new day God has given
you a new start! He is faithful, merciful, and loves you to life! Meditate
on His goodness today! Have an attitude of gratitude today! Thank
Him for the favor in your life today! Understanding that if it had not
been for the Lord by your side, where would you be? Thank you God*

You are blessed to be a Blessing!

> *My prayer for you today is that you will have an attitude
> of gratitude today and every day for the new mercy,
> favor, and grace that God so faithfully gives!*

Your scripture for today:

Isaiah 26:3-4

You will keep in perfect peace him whose mind is steadfast, because he trusts in you. Trust in the Lord forever, for the Lord, the Lord is the Rock eternal.

Observation:

This is a song of praise to the Lord for keeping our minds in perfect peace. But we have a part to play in it. We must focus on him instead of our problem. There is a peace that comes when we do. Worry is negative meditation, but when we magnify our God and seek his face, taking all the burdens and giving them to him our meditation is peaceful. Trust in the fact that he can, and will take care of your problems, because he cares about you. We can be in perfect peace just trust in God!

You are blessed to be a Blessing!

My prayer for you today is that you will keep your mind in perfect peace as you stay focused on the Lord!

May 16

Your scripture for today:

Matthew 11: 28-30

Come to me, all you who labor and are heavy laden, and I will give you rest. Take my yoke upon you and learn from me, for I am gentle and lowly in heart, and you will find rest for your souls. For my yoke is easy and my burden is light.

Observation:

Driving in the city I saw a homeless man carrying a lot of bags that must have been filled with his possessions. He was walking slowly and you could tell that the bags must have been heavy. It was plain to see that his things were important to him because no matter how heavy they were he was willing to carry the load. We all have things in our lives that we want to hold on to but they really have become heavy burdens. God is always reminding us to stop running ourselves crazy and cast all of your cares on Him. He wants you to come to him and ask for his assistance in everything you do. His ways are so much easier than what you can even think to do. You have to be willing to release the burden, let it go! All he asks is that you come to him learn from him and find the rest and peace that you need to succeed in every area of your life!

You are blessed to be a Blessing!

> *My prayer for you today is that you will*
> *give all your cares to the Lord!*

May 17

Your scripture for today:

Psalm 30:4-5

Sing to the Lord, you saints of his; praise his holy names. For his anger last only a moment, but his favor lasts a lifetime; weeping may remain for a night, but rejoicing comes in the morning.

Observation:

We may have setbacks and things in our past that rob us of our joy. Just keep in mind that as long as we don't continue to look back, we can move forward with God's everlasting favor. It's ok to cry and let it out just put a time limit on those tears because when the tears dry up you can look for the lesson in that obstacle. With every new morning comes a new opportunity to have joy, peace, love, and blessings. You will be stronger because you understand that trouble doesn't last always. So be encouraged, no matter what's going on!

You are blessed to be a Blessing!

My prayer for you today is that you get the lesson in the obstacle and get your joy back!

May 18

Your scripture for today:

Job 5:17-18

Blessed is the man whom God corrects; so do not despise the discipline of the Almighty. For he wounds, but he also binds up; he injures, but his hands also heal.

Observation:

A good parent will discipline and correct their child when they are headed to something that might hurt them. Just like any great parent Father God disciplines us to show us when we might be headed to destruction. Like a great coach discipline and corrects the player to bring out the best in them. God gives us correction to make us the best that he knows we can be. Although it may not be comfortable while the discipline is happening, when you look back you understand how it has helped you be a person of excellence living a life full of abundant blessings.

You are blessed to be a Blessing!

*My prayer for you today is that you expect and accept
the discipline and correction from God because it
will help you be the best that you can be!*

Your scripture for today:

Jeremiah 29:11

**"For I know the plans I have for you," declares
the Lord, "plans to prosper you and not to harm
you, plans to give you hope and a future."**

Observation:

*Have you ever bought something that you had to assemble? It usually
comes with directions inside. Which means the person or company
that created it put together the step by step plan to put what you
purchased together so that it does what it was created to do. In the
same way God has put together his plan and already mapped out the
things that he has for you. But he gave us freedom to choose our own
direction. You have to take the time to seek him first. He is your creator
and has your step by step instructions for a bright and hopeful future.*

You are blessed to be a Blessing!

*My prayer for you today is that you will understand that God has
an awesome plan for you and you can't do anything but be blessed!*

May 20

Your scripture for today:

2 Thessalonians 1:11-12

With this in mind, we constantly pray for you, that our God may count you worthy of his calling, and that by his power he may fulfill every purpose of yours and every act prompted by your faith. We pray this so that the name of our Lord Jesus may be glorified in you and you in him, according to the grace of our God and the Lord Jesus Christ.

Observation:

I hope it is clear that God wants you to succeed in every area of your lives because you are a reflection of him on earth! As he fulfills every purpose and act that you begin, others will want to know more about the God you serve. Make sure to take time to thank God for the blessings that he has already given to you knowing and believing that the best is yet to come! I really believe that God looks for consistency. This scripture is asking us to constantly or consistently pray. Whether your prayer is for someone you know or someone you don't know it's good to pray constantly. Then our purpose is fulfilled because we put or faith to work.

You are blessed to be a Blessing!

My prayer for you today is that you pray constantly for those in need and that God will help you succeed in every area of your life and all you touch will prosper!

May 21

Your scripture for today:

Psalms 52:8

**But as for me, I am like a green olive tree in the house of God;
I trust in the loving-kindness of God forever and ever.**

Observation:

*When others have turned away from God and it might even seem like
they are succeeding in their own power. Stay rooted and planted in the
house of God and following His will and plan for your life. Trust in His
unfailing love for you because you are His child and He will not guide
you down a path of destruction. Trust and know that your best is yet
to come. It will be rooted and grounded in love! It will not fail because
when God does it, it will exceed anything you could ask or think!*

You are blessed to be a Blessing!

*My prayer for you today is that you will be rooted
and ground in the love of the Lord!*

Your scripture for today:

Psalms 111:10

**The fear of the Lord is the beginning of wisdom;
all those who practice it have a good understanding.
His praise endures forever!**

Observation:

Wisdom starts by knowing and understanding that God created you, breathed life into you, and put you here for His purpose! As you acknowledge that truth you will begin to see all that God has for you. Your eyes will be opened to the supernatural wisdom that only He gives to those who love him and are called according to His purpose. This wisdom is better than any college degree can give you. This wisdom is from God who knows all and can lead and guide you to the life of abundance that he has already predestined you to have. Going to school is a good thing but remember there is no knowledge like the wisdom and knowledge you can receive from God.

You are blessed to be a Blessing!

*My prayer for you today is that you receive the
wisdom and knowledge that God so freely gives!*

May 23

Your scripture for today:

Isaiah 43:18-19

Forget the former things; do not dwell on the past. See, I am doing a new thing! Now it springs up; do you not perceive it? I am making a way in the desert and streams in the wasteland.

Observation:

I have seen people get stuck in the past! They had a great life in high school and when it was time to become an adult they never made that transition. They would relive the good old days of high school over and over because moving into the new adult life required too much effort. After all who wants to work and pay bills? It's easier to dwell on the past because it's familiar. What it boils done to is fear! Fear of the unknown can rob you of the blessings that God have for you. God is trying do a new thing in your life and you can't see it because of the routine of your everyday life! Realize that the new begins with a new mindset and attitude. Wake up each day open to receive all that God has for you not just accepting what you already have. Open your heart and eyes to the new that God has for you! Don't get stuck in the past the best is yet to come!

You are blessed to be a Blessing!

My prayer for you today is that you open your heart, eyes and arms to receive all the new things that God has for you!

Your scripture for today:

Philippians 1:6

Being confident of this, that he who began a good work in you will carry it on to completion until the day of Christ Jesus.

Observation:

I love to watch home improvement shows! They start out with a vision of how they want the project to look, than create the blueprint. The contractor hires the crew of experts to work on the various details of the plan. Once everyone has the vision and understands the plan the work begins. They tear out the old in order to begin the new design. As they begin to tear out the old it's inevitable that they find something wrong with the foundation, wiring or plumbing that was unexpected. You can have a vision and make the plan but obstacles will come. However, they always work it out and the project gets finished with amazing beauty! God has started a good work in you and he is going to finish it. He is not like man who starts things then changes his mind because of difficult times, or money looks funny, or the weather isn't perfect. No, God started the work in you and no matter what obstacles come he is finishing it so that you will stand in amazement of the finished project that he began and completed in you! You and others will see the new you and all they will be able to say is OH MY GOD!

You are blessed to be a Blessing!

My prayer for you today is that you allow God to finish the work in you. Be confident and sure that it will be done!

May 25

Your scripture for today:

Joel 2:25-26

I will repay you for the years the locusts have eaten~the great locust and the young locust, the other locust and locust swarm~my great army that I sent among you. You will have plenty to eat, until you are full, and you will praise the name of the Lord your God, who has worked wonders for you: never again will my people be shamed.

Observation:

Growing up in humble beginnings I have seen firsthand how God will bless and restore. Being seventh of nine children there was usually just enough to go around. I have seen how God will restore the years of lack back to you and give you years of plenty. There is nothing too hard for God. He is faithful and will work wonders for you! Think about the times *when everything went haywire.* Then understand that you have a new day of new beginnings and God is going to repay you double for your trouble. *You will have to give glory to God because it will be obvious that He did it.* Think of anything you can give thanks for and with that attitude of gratitude begin to give God thanks. No matter how small it may seem God can bless that! Those who are thankful are fruitful and those who are thankless are fruitless. Let's begin this new day with thanksgiving in our hearts! *Confident in the knowledge that restoration is your gift from God!*

You are blessed to be a Blessing!

My prayer for you today is that you will experience restoration from the Lord. Double blessing in every area of your life!

May 26

Your scripture for today:

John 5:19

Jesus gave them this answer: I tell you the truth, the Son can do nothing by himself; he can do only what he sees his Father doing, because whatever the Father does the Son also does.

Observation:

My Mom was an outstanding seamstress, interior decorator, and an awesome cook. With a large family she kept us dressed nice, a well-kept home with beautiful furnishings and the food was good! Because of her example I have a love for sewing, decorating and well the cooking is coming along with the help of the cooking channel! You are God's sons & daughters and He has provided and expects you to do what you have seen your Father do. That is amazing and puts us in a powerful place. Just like your children see what you do, God is your example because he is your Father. You can do all things because you are in the family. Get your confidence level up; expect the best because it's your birthright.

You are blessed to be a Blessing!

My prayer for you today is that you follow in the footsteps of your Father God and do all that he has for you to do!

May 27

Your scripture for today:

John 16:13

But when he, the Spirit of truth, comes, he will guide you into all truth. He will not speak on his own; he will speak only what he hears, and he will tell you what is yet to come.

Observation:

Think of the words that you speak out of your mouth as your declaration for what you want to see happen in your future! Would you change the things you talk about? When you speak you are predicting your future. God sent His Spirit to you to be a guide but you have a lot to do with that. The Spirit cannot guide you in a different direction then what you say out of your mouth. He does not take over your life and guide you in a different direction than what you are thinking about and speaking about. The Holy Spirit wants to help you be, do and have the things that God has set aside for you. That is why the scripture says do not grieve the Holy Spirit of God. (Ephesians 3:30) If you speak about negative things, lack, doubt, and put yourself down, you are telling the Spirit what to produce in your life. So, speak words of hope, faith, love, peace, and abundance at all times and watch as the Spirit go to work.

You are blessed to be a Blessing!

My prayer for you today is that you will begin to make powerful declarations of prosperity, health and peace for your future!

May 28

Your scripture for today:

Acts 16:25-26

About midnight Paul and Silas were praying and singing hymns to God, and the other prisoners were listening to them. Suddenly there was such a violent earthquake that the foundations of the prison were shaken. At once all the prison doors flew open, and every body's chains came loose.

Observation:

This is a perfect example of when the praises go up the blessing come down. Haven't you noticed that you gravitate to things that sound good? We all like it when someone gives us compliments or just says something nice about us. We bring God on the scene when we sing praises to him. He loves to hear our praise as we worship him in spirit and with our voice. When we come together in prayer there is so much power that even those just listening will become free of their chains as well. Where-ever you are you can start a movement for God. You can be the one to break the chains of discouragement at your workplace. You can be the one who brings God on the scene in your family. Where-ever there is a need to break the chains of bondage just begin to praise God because you should never underestimate the power we have when we pray and praise God. He will make everything right and suddenly in the midnight hour God will turn it around and work it out in your favor!

You are blessed to be a Blessing!

My prayer for you today is that you will sing praises to God so that He will shower you and all those around you with blessings!

May 29

Your scripture for today:

Proverbs 22:17-19

Pay attention and listen to the sayings of the wise; apply your heart to what I teach, for it is pleasing when you keep them in your heart and have all of them ready on your lips. So that your trust may be in the Lord.

Observation:

Sometimes the hardest things for us to do are pay attention and listen. God has given me the opportunity to be a trainer, teaching on different subjects about business. It's always noticeable when you finish training and someone comes to you and ask you for the answer to something you just finished training on. It was as if my words went in one ear and back out the other. The message was received but not retained. I have found that sometimes we have to hear things several times before it penetrates and sticks with you. We are so used to getting things quickly we don't have time to listen to wisdom. We mentally agree but don't allow it to penetrate to the heart. When we make the effort to read the word, or listen to a motivational CD in the car that helps us to store up the wisdom we need in our hearts which will eventually be what we begin to speak. Take some time today to pay attention and listen to what God has to say! Repeat it over and over again until it gets deep in your heart!

You are blessed to be a Blessing!

> *My prayer for you today is that you will listen to what God is speaking to you and that you will meditate on it so that it penetrates your heart!*

Your scripture for today:

Ecclesiastes 11:4-5

Whoever watches the wind will not plant; whoever looks at the clouds will not reap. As you do not know the path of the wind, or how the body is formed in a mother's womb, so you cannot understand the work of God, the Maker of all things.

Observation:

My Dad used to say, "Study long you study wrong". I used to wonder what he meant but I soon realized that in order to ever do anything different you have to be willing to step out in faith. If you look at anything too long and analyze every little detail you will never make a move. You ask everyone what they think and get 100 different views, when all you need is the viewpoint from the Lord. When He gives you a dream or vision just go for it. It is a new day and time so stop waiting on things to be totally right in your life before you act on the dreams and desires God has placed in your hearts. If you look at what's going on around you, you will never make a step to do anything different. Take a step of faith and trust that God's got your back.

You are blessed to be a Blessing!

My prayer for you today is that you will take the step of faith and move into the greatness that God has placed in you!

May 31

Your scripture for today:

Luke 19:46

'My house will be a house of prayer'

Observation:

I grew up going to church every Sunday. There were some members who would come early to have intercessory prayer before the service. They would pray over all the seats in the sanctuary and for those who were coming to church that day. They would pray that the lost would be saved that day and that those in need of healing would be healed that day. There was no doubt that our church was a house of prayer. As I got older I began to realize that the church isn't the only house where there should be prayer. Don't you know that you yourselves are God's temple and that God's Spirit dwells in your midst? (1 Corinthians 3:16) Therefore, you can be a prayer warrior at all times because God lives in you. But, you can also declare over your dwelling that it is a house of prayer, peace and joy! You can do just like the members did in the church house. You want your home to be a place where you are comfortable, love is flowing, everyone is healthy, and saved by the grace of God. It should be a place where you hear the sounds of laughter and singing. Make every effort to keep drama, strife and bitterness out of your home! Whether big or small, in the city or in country make yours a happy home filled with prayer, peace, love and joy!

You are blessed to be a Blessing!

> *My prayer for you today is that your house will be a*
> *house of prayer. As others enter into your home they*
> *will feel the love, peace and comfort of God!*

JUNE

June 1

Your scripture for today:

Proverbs 8:17

**I love them that love me; and those that
seek me early shall find me.**

Observation:

*Have you ever heard someone say or found yourself saying, "I guess all
I can do is pray?" You have exhausted everything possible and now as
a final straw it's time to seek God. It's true that God wants you to do
what is in your power to do. But the point is, when you seek Him first
he gives you wisdom and direction to get it done with ease and grace.
Realize that the answer you need is found in the Lord. The guidance
you seek comes from the Lord. The void in your life can be filled by
the Lord. Seek Him first and all these things will be added to your life.*

You are blessed to be a Blessing!

> *My prayer for you today is that prayer is the
> first thing you think to do every day!*

June 2

Your scripture for today:

Matthew 18:19-20

**Again, I tell you that if two of you on earth agree
about anything you ask for, it will be done for you
by my father in heaven. For where two or three come
together in my name there am I with them.**

Observation:

*For more than 10 years I have been a part of a 6:00 am prayer
conference call. When I first started the call there were quite a few
ladies who would call in. It was amazing praying for all the needs of
the people. After a while many stopped calling in because that 6:00 am
time was truly a sacrifice. So for the last few years we have 5 powerful
prayer warriors who are faithful and have a passion for interceding for
others. We have seen so many of our prayers answered that it is really
amazing! We have people who know about our call and ask for us to
pray for them. The power of agreement is awesome. Having a prayer
partner or in my case prayer partners it is a wonderful thing. When
you can come together for one common purpose and lift up the name
of Jesus. When you bring your energy and they bring theirs, it brings
God on the scene double time. He hears your prayers, so believe that it's
already done while you are praying and you will have it. It's a dynamic,
energizing experience to pray together and see it come to pass!*

You are blessed to be a Blessing!

*My prayer for you today is that you will understand the power of
prayer and having prayer partners! Where 2 or 3 are gathered in
Jesus name he is there to hear your prayer and meet your needs!*

Your scripture for today:

Deuteronomy 8:17-18

**You may say to yourself, "My power and the strength
of my hands have produced this wealth for me." But
remember the Lord your God, for it is he who gives you the
ability to produce wealth, and so confirms his covenant,
which he swore to your forefathers, as it is today.**

Observation:

*God has blessed you to be prosperous in this life and to live a life of
abundance. He has given you everything you need to succeed. All he
wants is to be remembered for what he has given you. Imagine how you
would feel if you were a major help in the success of someone and they
never said thank you or even acknowledged what you did. Give honor
to which honor is due and be grateful for all that God has done and
is doing in your life. Just recognize His spiritual power that's leading
and guiding you and always give God the glory!*

You are blessed to be a Blessing!

*My prayer for you today is that you remember the
Lord when your blessings begin to flow!*

Your scripture for today:

Psalm 107:8-9

**Let them give thanks to the Lord for his unfailing love
and his wonderful deeds for men, for he satisfies the
thirsty and fills the hungry with good things.**

Observation:

*God is good to us and he loves us unconditionally. He is our rock, our
provider, our Lord, our Savior, our redeemer and our deliverer. He
makes a way out of no way. He heals our bodies, and gives us eternal
life. Have you ever been thirsty and needed to get a drink? All you
can think of is getting something to drink. In the same way; when the
hunger pangs hit, your mind is set on getting something to eat as soon
as possible. God is here to satisfy your every need. Be thankful for all
that He has done and is doing in you. Stay hungry for God and He
will continue to provide a buffet of blessings for you! With Him you
can have it all!*

You are blessed to be a Blessing!

> *My prayer for you today is that you will
> stay thirsty and hungry for God!*

June 5

Your scripture for today:

2 Kings 6:16-17

"'Don't be afraid,' the prophet answered. 'Those who are with us are more than those who are with them.' And Elisha prayed, 'O Lord, open his eyes so he may see.' Then the Lord opened the servant's eyes, and he looked and saw the hills full of horses and chariots of fire all around Elisha."

Observation:

Our false perception is the biggest cause of fear and frustration! If you live without faith, your perception is restricted to what you see with your eyes and hear with your ears. With this limited input, it's easy to live in fear. Therefore, many become frustrated and discouraged with their day to day life. But as your faith and understanding of God increase, you are able to trust in what you cannot physically see or hear. God will open your eyes to see all that He has for you, just believe!

You are blessed to be a Blessing!

My prayer for you today is that you will open your eyes to all the possibilities that God has for you! You don't have to be afraid of anything!

Your Scripture for today:

Proverbs 31:29-30

**"Many women do noble things,
but you surpass them all."
Charm is deceptive, and beauty is fleeting;
but a woman who fears the LORD is to be praised.**

Observation:

Most women are great at multi-tasking to get things done and make it look easy. What a special gift that God gave to all women to make sure the family's needs would be met. There is a lot to be said about a good women; she is praised where ever she goes. She takes care of herself, making sure her outer appearance is outstanding. But the most outstanding thing that is apparent to all is that she fears the Lord! Beauty is only skin deep, and wearing fashionable clothing can get you nice compliments. But the woman who has wisdom, knowledge and understanding from God is anointed and irresistible. She draws people to her because of her positive energy and outlook on life. Fear the Lord and be praised!

You are blessed to be a Blessing!

*My prayer for all women is that you will seek the Lord
and His awesomeness and you will be praised!*

June 7

Your scripture for today:

Isaiah 59:1

**Surely the arm of the LORD is not too short to save,
nor his ear too dull to hear.**

Observation:

*Through depression, loneliness, and low self-esteem, the Lord is able to
deliver you. When you are crying and reaching out for help, the Lord is
able to hear and save you. God hears your whisper! Many people will
never experience what you have experienced in life. Some would never
recover from what you endured. God hears you when your body is tired
and your voice is weak. He is able to hear what no one else hears. He is
able to be strong when you are weak. Don't ever feel like you are alone
because God has promised to never leave you or forsake you. Be strong
and courageous. Do not be afraid or terrified because of them, for the
LORD your God goes with you; he will never leave you nor forsake you."
(Deuteronomy 31:6) God is a good God, and you are #1 in His book!*

You are blessed to be a Blessing!

*My prayer for you today is that you will know the
goodness of God first hand and understand that he
is always with and will never forsake you!*

June 8

Your scripture for today:

John 15:5

**I am the vine; you are the branches. If a man
remains in me and I in him, he will bear much
fruit; apart from me you can do nothing.**

Observation:

*Have you ever tried to do something in your own power and got
frustrated and confused? Or have you ever been determined to get
into a relationship with someone who you thought was the right one,
ignoring all the warning signs that God was throwing your way?
Remember that whatever you do apart from God you have to maintain
apart from God. Life does not have to be that hard! So when you stay
close to God, your source, you are able to do powerful and amazing
things. You get the wisdom, discernment, grace and peace that come
from the vine. The key is to be led by the Spirit of God and you will do
all things and bear much fruit!*

You are blessed to be a Blessing!

*My prayer for you today is that you will know that the
closer you get to God the more fruit you will bear!*

June 9

Your scripture for today:

Psalm 62:11

One thing God has spoken, two things have I heard; that you, O God, are strong, and that you, O Lord, are loving. Surely you will reward each person according to what he has done.

Observation:

We serve a strong and loving God who wants us to be all, do all, and have it all! He is a rewarder of those who seek him that do his word and have compassion. What have you done lately to help someone in need? That person in need could be you. Have you done anything special for yourself lately? You are the temple of God, so take some time out for you. You have to fill yourself up so that you can give out to someone else. As they say on the airplane, 'Put the oxygen mask on you first then help someone else in need.' Do something good for you today!

You are blessed to be a Blessing!

My prayer for you today is that you be rewarded for all the good you do and that you will also take the time to be good to yourself!

June 10

Your scripture for today:

Joshua 1:9

**Have I not commanded you? Be strong and courageous.
Do not be afraid; do not be discouraged, for the LORD
your God will be with you wherever you go."**

Observation:

Discouragement is one of the enemies most used tools. He is able to pry open and get inside your heart with that tool when he can't get near you with any other. Recognize and understand his tricks and laugh in the face of whatever adversity or discouragement he is trying to bring your way. Laugh because God is in control of your life. He will be with you wherever you go and whatever you do. Disappointed laugh, discouraged laugh, obstacles laugh, because you know God is with you and this too shall pass!

You are blessed to be a Blessing!

My prayer for you today is that you will be able to laugh through any disappointment, discouragement, or obstacles that come your way because you know that God has got it all under control!

Your scripture for today:

Deuteronomy 10:21

He is the one you praise; he is your God, who performed for you those great and awesome wonders you saw with your own eyes.

Observation:

God has shown up time and time again in our lives and is always faithful. You must begin to praise the things that He has done and not take it for granted. You have seen Him change things for the better when it looked like you had no way out. Don't get it twisted and think that you need to praise someone else for the blessings in your life. It was God that made it happen. He may be behind the scenes working on your behalf even when you can›t see it *initially! But trust and believe that it will all work out for your good. God has already walked out your footsteps; he knows the obstacles you will face and every test that you will have to pass. You have witnessed His goodness before so praise Him at all times!*

You are blessed to be a Blessing!

> *My prayer for your today is that you remember that God has brought you out and given you the victory so give him all the praise, glory, and honor he deserves!*

June 12

Your scripture for today:

Lamentations 3:25-26

**The LORD is good to those whose hope is in him,
to the one who seeks him;
it is good to wait quietly
for the salvation of the LORD.**

Observation:

Have you ever found yourself in a situation where you needed help or answers for something? When you are sick and go to the doctor you are hoping that you can get answers to whatever is going on. You went there seeking the Doctor for what you need. Usually you get to the office, check in, and then wait in the lobby until your name is called. When the nurse comes and calls your name they usher you in the examining room, take some vitals, like temperature, blood pressure, and weight. Then the nurse leaves and you wait quietly for the Doctor to come hoping that he has the answer. Well, this is how you should be with God. Seeking Him out and waiting patiently for His salvation. While you wait keep hoping for the best that God has for you! So when you are in that Doctors office, pray and hope that God gives him the wisdom to know exactly how to help you with your situation. God is faithful so seek Him and put your hope in His salvation!

You are blessed to be a Blessing!

*My prayer for you today is that you always hope in
the Lord and patiently wait for His salvation!*

June 13

Your scripture for today:

Psalm 34:12-14

**Whoever of you loves life and desires to see many good days,
keep your tongue from evil and your lips from speaking lies.
Turn from evil and do good; seek peace and pursue it.**

Observation:

*Have you ever known someone who lies about everything? I knew
someone like that. They would lie even when the truth would have
sounded better. I knew a lie was about to come out when they would
close their eyes before they started to speak. It was like they were
thinking up the next lie they were going to tell! There can't be any peace
in that! How can you keep all the lies straight? God wants to satisfy
you with long life! You just need to praise him and understand that
he seeks to satisfy you. When you seek peace and not drama, when
you speak the truth and love one another, when you desire to do good
to others you not only extend your life but also leave a great legacy of
peace, goodness, and love that will live on.*

You are blessed to be a Blessing!

*My prayer for you today is that you pursue peace, love and
truth today and live the long life that God has for you!*

June 14

Your scripture for today:

Ephesians 3:20

**Now to Him who is able to do exceedingly abundantly
above all that we ask or think, according to the
power that works in us, to Him be glory...**

Observation:

*God is not just able to do beyond what we ask, but abundantly beyond.
But that's not enough; He is able to do exceedingly abundantly beyond
what we ask. Now, what is it that you need? Build up your faith so that
God can work with the power within you to make it come to pass. Get
outrageous with your faith and ask God to do far beyond what you
can think. God doesn't deal with addition unless that's as far as your
faith will allow you to see. God deals with multiplication. He said
he will multiply your seed so, while you are dreaming, dream bigger
than you can imagine or think! That's when God steps in. He puts the
supernatural favor on it so that you can't do anything but know that
it had to be God. You have not because you ask not. Just make sure to
give Him the glory, honor and praise!*

You are blessed to be a Blessing!

*My prayer for you today is that you will have
supernatural, exceedingly and abundant blessings
and give God all the glory, honor and praise!*

June 15

Your scripture for today:

Colossians 4:2

Devote yourself to prayer, being watchful and thankful.

Observation:

When you pray it's just communication with God. You can tell Him all about your troubles, your heartache, your pain, and you can even tell Him about all that you are excited about. Think of it as if you are talking with your best friend. What would you tell them? Wouldn't you tell them about everything? The difference is that you can see and touch your friend on earth. However, your friend on earth has limited wisdom and knowledge about what's best for you. There are times however that God can drop a word of wisdom to your friend because he wanted to get a message to you. But when you are devoted to prayer you are always allowing God's power to enter the situation. You can pray while you drive, pray while you walk, pray as you walk into work, pray when you can't figure things out. Just talking to him about any and everything. It doesn't have to be with a lot of words. It can be as simple as "God I need your help" or, "Thank you God for all that you do" whatever you decide to say, just pray!

You are blessed to be a Blessing!

> *My prayer for you today is that you will pray without ceasing until you receive your blessings and then offer a prayer of thanksgiving for the abundance in your life!*

June 16

Your scripture for today:

Psalm 18:16-19

**He reached down from on high and took hold of me;
he drew me out of deep waters. He rescued me from my
powerful enemy, from my foes, who were too strong for
me. They confronted me in the day of my disaster, but the
Lord was my support. He brought me out into a spacious
place; he rescued me because he delighted in me.**

Observation:

*Have you ever had to come to the rescue of a child? Like any good
parent we will pick them up and reassure them that everything will
be alright. The tears stop but you might have to hold them for a little
while. Well that is exactly what God does for us. You are his child, he
delights in you and he supports you! No matter what is coming against
you, He reaches down from on high and takes hold of you. You will be
lifted up to higher places because of your loving Father God!*

You are blessed to be a Blessing!

*My prayer for you today is that you will know that your heavenly
father is madly in love with you. He is concerned about you and will
protect you from the enemy. You are strong because he is strong!*

June 17

Your scripture for today:

Psalm 30:5

For His anger *is but for* a moment, His favor *is for* life; Weeping may endure for a night, but joy *comes* in the morning.

Observation:

Remember when you got so angry about something that you didn't think you would ever get past it? You might get angry with a co-worker or maybe it was your spouse or child. Does it last forever? Was it worth getting your blood pressure up? Sometimes in the heat of the anger you might say things that you regret later or do things that afterward you wish you had not done. It's always good to remember this passage of scripture. Learn to walk away and cool off! Gather your thoughts and ask yourself what would Jesus do? Thank God that His anger is but for a moment when we do things that grieve Him. It's good to know that his mercy is new every morning. You may have times that it seems everything is coming against you. As if God is angry with you. But just know that God doesn't hold on to your past mistakes or failures. He is slow to anger and quick to forgive. You are always covered by His love, favor, mercy and grace. So get your joy back and rejoice it's a new day!

You are blessed to be a Blessing!

My prayer for you todays: Lord let your Spirit of peace and understanding live big within and allow us to be slow to anger and quick to forgive. Remind us Lord that weeping may endure for a night but joy will come in the morning light!

June 18

Your scripture for today:

1 John 4:4

You, dear children, are from God and have overcome them, because the one who is in you is greater than the one who is in the world.

Observation:

The Spirit of God is in us flowing through our bodies and giving us insight in all things. But there are times when we allow others to get us upset and rattled because of their actions or lack of action, because of their words, or lack of words. Their likes or dislikes. That is when we need to step away from it, let go of it and allow God to work it out. We are overcomers because God created us and gave us his spirit to make sure of it! Don't sweat the small stuff! God's got it all under control!

You are blessed to be a Blessing!

> *My prayer for you today: God give strength to those who are weak today. Give them the confidence to know that they are overcomers because you have it all under control!*

June 19

Your scripture for today:

Luke 5:4-6

When he had finished speaking, he said to Simon, "Put out into deep water, and let down the nets for a catch." Simon answered, "Master, we've worked hard all night and haven't caught anything. But because you say so, I will let down the nets." When they had done so, they caught such a large number of fish that their nets began to break.

Observation:

Just when you think you've done everything you can do and it's time to give up on your dream God says do it again! The only difference this time is that HE said do it again! When his anointing is on it your seed will be multiplied. Don't lean on your own understanding because you may not understand it but He said it, so be it! You might even have a college degree in the specific area. But Gods knowledge is supernatural and He controls it all. So no matter what it looks like in the natural, just trust in the directive He gives you. Now it's time to go deeper, cast more than one net, explore new territories. You'll have favor, and break through success!

You are blessed to be a Blessing!

My prayer for you today is that as the Lord gives the orders you will obey and follow your supernatural leading!

June 20

Your scripture for today:

Mark 13:35-37

**Therefore keep watch because you do not know when the
owner of the house will come back whether in evening,
or at midnight, or when the rooster crows, or at dawn.
If he comes suddenly, do not let him find you sleeping.
What I say to you, I say to everyone: 'Watch!'**

Observation:

*Have your ever planned a party to have at your home? You make
sure everything is just right because you want to be ready when your
company arrives. If you wait until the last minute it can get rather
hectic, rushed, and anxiety can set in. We know that God is coming
back and even though we don't know the date or time, we can keep
things in order because God wants you to always be ready for his
return. You can do some basic cleaning like forgiving others, repenting
of sin, and walking in love to others. By acknowledging Him as Lord of
your life and keeping your Spirit clean you will be ready for His return.*

You are blessed to be a Blessing!

*My prayer for you today is that you will clean your spiritual
house in preparation of God's return every day!*

June 21

Your scripture for today:

Psalm 5:11-12

But let all who take refuge in you be glad; let them ever sing for joy. Spread your protection over them that those who love your name may rejoice in you. For surely, O Lord, you bless the righteous; you surround them with your favor as with a shield.

Observation:

When you need to take refuge it's because you are displaced for some reason. You have no home to go to therefore you are in need of shelter and protection. God has clearly promised us to be our ever-present help in times of trouble (Psalm 46:1). He has promised to bless us and give us His favor. Did you put on your Crown of Favor this morning? Did you forget who you are? It's not too late to put it on because you are a child of God and you have his protection love and favor! Believe that God is on your side. Where ever you are remember that He has surrounded you with his favor as you go about your day. Put your shoulders back and head up so your crown doesn't fall. Take some time to thank Him for His goodness and rejoice!

You are blessed to be a Blessing!

My prayer for you today is that you will always remember that you have Gods favor all over you! He has you surrounded with his favor like a shield!

June 22

Your scripture for today:

Galatians 5:14-15

The entire law is summed up in a single command: "Love your neighbor as yourself." If you keep on biting and devouring each other, watch out or you will be destroyed by each other.

Observation:

God has placed in us the ability to love. We also have the ability to hate. When we realize that everyone is made in the image of God and that he is love, it is obvious how we should be treating our fellow man. Examine your heart and make sure you are walking in love and not hate. When your neighbor, brother, sister, or whoever gets blessed, don't hate, congratulate! You are a child of God just like they are, so be happy for them. God will reward you because you let love prevail!

You are blessed to be a Blessing!

My prayer for you today is that you will walk in love each and every day! That you will be able to be happy for the blessings that others receive knowing that you are in the same line to be blessed by God!

June 23

Your scripture for today:

Philippians 4:13

I can do everything through him who gives me strength.

Observation:

God has given you everything you need to be able to succeed in life. He has given you the power to obtain wealth. He has given you dreams and desires to get you to the purpose that you are here for. He has given you his spirit to strengthen and guide you. Now it is up to you to take the first step and allow him to move in your life. Being confident in who you are and calling on your heavenly Father for guidance. Be strong; don't give away your power by giving into fear. Have faith and be willing to take a risk, you can do it, because you have the power!

You are blessed to be a Blessing!

> *My prayer for you today is that you know the truth about your heavenly Father because he will strengthen you with his power to do amazing things. I pray that you get your confidence up and know that you can do all things with God!*

June 24

Your scripture for today:

Psalm 138:1-3 (Message)

Thank you! Everything in me says "Thank you!" Angels listen as I sing my thanks. I kneel in worship facing your holy temple and say it again: "Thank you!" Thank you for your love, thank you for your faithfulness; most holy is your name, most holy is your Word. The moment I called out, you stepped in; you made my life large with strength.

Observation:

With an attitude of gratitude God can and will enter your life and give you strength to handle any situation! Thanksgiving is an everyday thing not once a year! Really look at what you have right now and think about the alternative. What if you didn't have that job that you complain about? What about those kids that might be getting on your last nerve! Be thankful with little and God will strengthen you and increase you! I started a gratitude journal years ago to remind myself every night of at least 5 things I am grateful for. It's a great way to end the day and make your sleep sweet. Thank God consistently and on purpose because he will also bless you consistently and on purpose!

Thank you God!

You are blessed to be a Blessing!

My prayer for you today and every day is that you find something to be thankful for! In the midst of the day consciously take time to just say thank you!

June 25

Your scripture for today:

Exodus 3:14

**God said to Moses, "I-AM-WHO-I-AM. Tell the
People of Israel, 'I-AM sent me to you.'"**

Observation:

*Who does God need to be for you? He is whoever you need Him to
be! He is your creator, your provider, your healer, your deliverer, and
your protector. He is a Father to the fatherless. God is your strength,
your hope, and your peace! When you have prayed and asked God
for direction, He will give you the wisdom and knowledge to do it.
Remember that God is in you residing on the inside of you. He left
His Spirit to help lead and guide you through this life. So be careful
what you say after "I AM" because you are declaring what you are. If
you say 'I am broke' in the natural that might be the case, but you are
speaking that into your life. Confess what you want to see instead of
what you don't want. Remind yourself that God will supply all your
needs according to His riches. God is in you and he said 'I Am' so that
means 'You Are'. You are more than a conqueror, you are blessed and
highly favored, you are the righteousness of God, and you are a child
of Almighty God! Go with confidence because "I AM" has sent you!*

You are blessed to be a Blessing!

> *My prayer for you today is that you will know who
> YOU ARE because I AM has sent you!*

June 26

Your scripture for today:

2 Chronicles 14:11

Then Asa called to the Lord his God and said, "Lord, there is no one like you to help the powerless against the mighty. Help us, Lord our God, for we rely on you, and in your name we have come against this vast army. Lord, you are our God; do not let mere mortals prevail against you."

Observation:

When you know who to call on in times of trouble you will win every time! God will fight your battles for you, all you have to do is ask Him, rely on Him and believe that He already has done it for you! When it seems that so much is coming against you and your problems are over your head just remember that it's under God's feet! Nothing's too hard or too big that God can't handle for you! Believe it, declare it, and God will prove it to you!

You are blessed to be a Blessing!

My prayer for you today is that you will call on God for all that you are in need of! Lord fight the battle of all your children today!

June 27

Your scripture for today:

Nehemiah 13:14

Remember me, O my God, for this. Don't ever forget the devoted work I have done for The Temple of God and its worship.

Observation:

We all want to be remembered for what we do. When you are recognized for your service it inspires you to do more because you feel appreciated! You may faithfully serve in your church or devote your time to a charity. God remembers you and is always reminded of you because the people you are serving are thanking Him for you. He is constantly hearing your name. Be encouraged today and know that your service is not in vain. You are leaving a legacy of good works for others to follow. Just know that the work you do for the Lord will always be remembered. When you touch the lives of others because of your service it will never be forgotten. Continue to serve and use the gift that God gave you!

You are blessed to be a Blessing!

My prayer for you today is that you will continue to serve using the gift that God gave you to bless others! You will leave a legacy of good works that will live on and on and on!

Your scripture for today:

Joshua 1:5-6

No one will be able to stand against you all the days of your life. As I was with Moses, so I will be with you; I will never leave you nor forsake you. Be strong and courageous, because you will lead these people to inherit the land I swore to their ancestors to give them.

Observation:

When you are called to be a leader you need to be encouraged to step up and be strong. Leaders can face opposition, criticism, and defiance from those that they have been chosen to lead. But when God has given you as the leader a vision He also gives you the provision to do it. You have to be strong and courageous to withstand all that may come against you. Don't look to the right or the left. Stay with it and you and your people will inherit what God has promised!

You are blessed to be a Blessing!

My prayer for you today is that you will be encouraged to keep going. God give them the strength to continue to lead those you have chosen to be led by the leader reading this prayer right now. Bless them and help them to know that you will never leave them or forsake them! Help them to know that they will obtain the promise!

June 29

Your scripture for today:

Haggai 2:9

The glory of this present house will be greater than the glory of the former house,' says the Lord Almighty. 'And in this place I will grant peace,' declares the Lord Almighty."

Observation:

As you move into the promises that God has for you the enemy will try to stop you from obtaining the best that God has for you! He will use devious tactics, discouragement, depression, and even the people you think are your friends to get you off track. When God moves you to a new place in life He is setting you up for greater victories. You have to hold on and be strong in the Lord and the power of his might. You will be abundantly blessed and most of all receive the peace of God that passes all understanding.

You are blessed to be a Blessing!

My prayer for you today is that the Lord will give you all that you have been promised and that you will recognize the tricks of the enemy that comes to steal, kill and destroy!

Your scripture for today:

Psalm 91:14-16

"Because he loves me," says the Lord, "I will rescue him; I will protect him, for he acknowledges my name. He will call on me, and I will answer him; I will be with him in trouble, I will deliver him and honor him. With long life I will satisfy him and show him my salvation."

Observation:

A friend of mine took a trip that was all inclusive. This was her first time taking a trip like this and was so excited to report how pampered she felt. The staff at the hotel catered to their every need and made sure they were taken care of. They wanted for nothing the entire time they were there! Well that is exactly how God is with us. God knows who his children are and is always there in times of trouble. You can lean on and trust in the fact that God is your protector and deliverer. Whatever you may be facing it did not come to stay, it came to pass. Look for the treasure in the trial because your biggest victory is about to be revealed. He is an all-inclusive God ready to cater to your every need. Continue to love the Lord God with all your heart and soul. He's got so much in store for you!

You are blessed to be a Blessing!

My prayer for you today is that you understand that you have a God that will pamper you, cater to you, protect you and make sure you want for nothing! Amen

JULY

Your scripture for today:

Lamentations 3:22-23

**Because of the Lord's great love we are not consumed,
for his compassions never fail. They are new
every morning; great is your faithfulness.**

Observation:

Whatever is going on in your life will not take over your life unless you allow it to. God always provides a way out. When He closes a door there is a window open for you to go through. Today is a new day! Thank God that with every new day He gives you new blessings, mercy, grace, and compassion! Yesterday is old news! The good news is that God is faithful and able to turn your mourning into dancing! Don't rehearse the problems of your pass or talk about the trouble you may be facing. Think about and reflect on your victories and how faithful God has been to you! Get your joy back and praise God because your best is yet to come!

You are blessed to be a Blessing!

*My prayer for you today is that you will praise God
no matter what it looks like. Remember your joy will
be renewed and God will see you through it.*

Your scripture for today is:

Philippians 4:6-7

Do not be anxious about anything, but in everything by prayer and supplication with thanksgiving let your requests be made known to God. And the peace of God, which surpasses all understanding, will guard your hearts and your minds in Christ Jesus.

Observation:

When you start to feel frustrated and out of control, just know that you are in need of God's intervention. When you believe that God is a God who can and has supplied your every need, you realize that you don't have to worry or be anxious about anything. He has already walked out your footsteps and knows exactly what you need before you do! When you make your request known to God through prayer, then meditate on Him, the Peace of God will flow all over and through you like being under a rain shower. Let His peace flow from the top of your head to the soles of your feet and thank God for all He has done and is doing in you! You have so much to be thankful for and your best is still yet to come.

You are blessed to be a Blessing!

My prayer for you today is that you will ask for God to intervene in all your affairs in life. Don't worry or be frustrated just pray to the Lord and He will bless the mess!

July 3

Your scripture for today:

Psalm 34:3-4

**Magnify the Lord with me! Let's praise his name together!
I sought the Lord's help and he answered me;
he delivered me from all my fears.**

Observation:

I love to travel and on one of my trips I had the window seat. As I stared out the window when the plane was taking off I thought about how everything begin to get smaller the higher up we went. That reminded me of how when you take you cares up to God and magnify Him instead of the problem they become smaller and smaller until they are no longer in sight. Instead of murmuring and complaining with others about the problems, talk about the goodness of GOD! Because he is so good all the time it makes you want to shout for joy! He said He rewards all those who diligently seek after Him. So when you need help, seek Him! When you need direction, seek Him! When you need wisdom in any situation, seek Him! And when fear tries to overtake you, seek Him, and you will be delivered! Magnify the Lord with me today!

You are blessed to be a Blessing!

My prayer for you today: Lord give the answers needed to deliver them from anything that comes their way. Magnify yourself to them so that all they can do is talk about you and not the problem!

Your scripture for today:

Malachi 3:16-17

Then those who feared the Lord spoke to one another, And the Lord listened and heard them; So a book of remembrance was written before Him For those who fear the Lord And who meditate on His name. "They shall be mine," says the Lord of hosts, "On the day that I make them my jewels. And I will spare them as a man spares his own son who serves him."

Observation:

Every morning my prayer partners and I get on our conference call and talk about Gods word. We speak of his goodness, thank him for the all that He has done and for all the blessings and increase still to come. God loves to hear the praises of His children! Any parent loves to hear their children say great things about them. It makes them want to do anything for them! Well God keeps a journal of all those who love Him, praise Him, believe in Him, serve Him, and meditate on Him. He sees every random act of kindness and everything that you have sacrificed for Him is being recorded. You are God's treasured possession and He will reward you abundantly!

You are blessed to be a Blessing!

My prayer for you today is; God help your people to speak more about you and thank you for all that you have done. Add them to your book of remembrance and continue to bless them!

July 5

Your scripture for today:

Psalm 23:4

**Yea, though I walk through the valley of the shadow
of death, I will fear no evil; For You *are* with me;
Your rod and Your staff, they comfort me.**

Observation:

*Living in Texas the rainstorms can be severe. I was driving on the
highway one day during one of storms and I noticed some cars had
pulled over to the side of the road because the rain was coming too
hard. But I decided to keep going because I could see that the sky was
lighter in a distance. As I drove about a mile more the rain had totally
stopped and the pavement wasn't even wet. But when I looked in the
rearview mirror it was still dark and raining just as hard. Thank God
I kept going! When you find yourself in a valley, keep walking! Don't
set up camp by murmuring and complaining about the valley. Don't
pitch a tent and analyze the valley. Keep walking! Even when all
kinds of shadows try to overtake you, remember you have the power
of the Holy Spirit with you. Power walk through that situation with
confidence! Speak positive words, know that God has already walked
out your footsteps and made your crooked places straight. Your best
is yet to come!*

You are blessed to be a Blessing!

*My prayer for you today is, Lord help them to keep it moving
during the hard times that come. There is light at the end of the
tunnel. Move toward the light of God and you will be blessed!*

Your scripture for today:

Psalm 37:23-24

The Lord makes firm the steps of the one who delights in him; though he may stumble, he will not fall, for the Lord upholds him with his hand.

Observation:

When a child is just starting to walk their steps are very unsure. They may even stumble and fall but they get back up and try again. All along the parent is walking behind them to make sure they don't hurt themselves. I also reminded of teaching my daughter how to ride her bike. She was very wobbly when the training wheels first came off. But I helped to steady her for a while until she finally got her balance then I let go and she rode by herself. I will never forget how excited she was when she realized she was doing it on her own. That's how God wants to lead you through this life! You might be a little wobbly or stumble but He will lead you to victory after victory! Even when you mess up, He will still be with you and give you grace, mercy and favor. Your mess will become your message to help others see the goodness of God!

You are blessed to be a Blessing!

My prayer for you today is that you will always remember that God is with you leading and guiding your footsteps. Get excited because he will never let you fall.

Your scripture for today:

Proverbs 25:21-22

If your enemy is hungry, give him bread to eat; and if he is thirsty, give him water to drink; for *so* you will heap coals of fire on his head, and the LORD will reward you.

Observation:

Because you are a child of God there is an anointing on you and your life that will cause some people to love you and others to hate you. When you enter a room you bring the light of God with you and those who are in the dark want to dim that light! But God's anointing is so powerful that His marvelous light will shine brighter because you are able to look pass their hate and be great anyway! Pray for those who persecute you because your reward comes from God!

You are blessed to be a Blessing!

My prayer for you today is that you will be great no matter what the haters think! Let your greatness be known because God is bringing it out of you so shine on!

July 8

Your scripture for today:

Proverbs 22: 17-19

Pay attention and turn your ear to the sayings of the wise; apply your heart to what I teach, for it is pleasing when you keep them in your heart and have all of them ready on your lips.

Observation:

In the Bible, Solomon had riches beyond compare. He could have anything he wanted, do whatever he wanted, and still not lack for anything. But when he was asked what he wanted he asked for wisdom!

Songs of Solomon 1:8-12

Solomon answered God, "You have shown great kindness to David my father and have made me king in his place. ⁹Now, LORD *God, let your promise to my father David be confirmed, for you have made me king over a people who are as numerous as the dust of the earth. ¹⁰Give me wisdom and knowledge, that I may lead this people, for who is able to govern this great people of yours?"¹¹ God said to Solomon, "Since this is your heart's desire and you have not asked for wealth, possessions or honor, nor for the death of your enemies, and since you have not asked for a long life but for wisdom and knowledge to govern my people over whom I have made you king, ¹²therefore wisdom and knowledge will be given you. And I will also give you wealth, possessions and honor, such as no king who was before you ever had and none after you will have."*

When you have the wisdom of God in your life there is nothing that can compare to it! It will keep you out of trouble, show you where to get the best deals, let you know who is for you and who is not! Seek wisdom and understanding from your creator God and you will be rich beyond compare!

You are blessed to be a Blessing!

My prayer for you today is that you will ask for wisdom, knowledge and understanding that only God can give!

Your scripture for today:

Jeremiah 42:6

**Whether it is good or bad, we will obey the voice of the Lord
our God to whom we are sending you that it may be well
with us when we obey the voice of the Lord our God."**

Observation:

*Knowing the voice of the Lord is crucial! There are many voices that
will try to speak into your life, but you need to know God's voice to
discern whether it is your God or the enemy. Spend time with God and
meditate on His words. Then when you hear something that doesn't
line up with the word of the Lord you will know that it is not God. He
said "I wish above all things that you would prosper and be in health,
even as your soul prospers!" Spend time in meditation with God learn
His voice. It's usually not a big boisterous voice like the Wizard of Oz!
It can be so quiet that if you aren't careful you will miss it. Shut down
some of noise around you and get in tune with the Father. Study and
know his voice so that it will be well with you!*

You are blessed to be a blessing!

*My prayer for you today is that you listen for the
voice of the lord! Get to know him by studying His
word and spending time with the Father!*

Your scripture for today:

John 1:1-3

In the beginning was the Word, and the Word was with God, and the Word was God. The same was in the beginning with God. All things were made by him; and without him was not anything made that was made.

Observation:

I love starting out my day with prayer, meditation, and the word of God. It's like hanging out and talking with your Creator. I am always amazed at the inspiration I receive from the Holy Spirit that gives me what to say in the Daily Word that I email too many people every week day. There is a promise in the word for every problem you may have. There is an entire book of wisdom in Proverbs. There are songs of praises and there are so many examples of miracles performed by God that He is still performing today! His grace, mercy, and favor are new every morning what a great way to begin your day!

You are blessed to be a Blessing!

> *My prayer for you today is that you will start your*
> *day with the word of God! It will bless your day!*

Your scripture for today:

Matthew 6:7-8

And when you pray, do not keep on babbling like pagans, for they think they will be heard because of their many words. ⁸ Do not be like them, for your Father knows what you need before you ask him.

Observation:

Prayer is like talking to a friend that knows you really well. They already know what you are going through and have compassion for the situation you may be in. You don't have to repeat it to them over and over because you know they already know and understand how you feel. Well, God is your creator and has walked out your footsteps before you were formed in your mother's womb. He knew where you would be right now and is not surprised! He just wants you to come to Him and give Him your permission to intervene and make things right! So have a little talk with Jesus today, He will make it alright!

You are blessed to be a Blessing!

My prayer for you today is that you will have a talk with Jesus because He is the best friend you would ever have! He already knows what you are going through and has the answer you need!

Your scripture for today:

Romans 13:8

**Let no debt remain outstanding, except the
continuing debt to love one another, for he who
loves his fellowman has fulfilled the law.**

Observation:

*When it comes to money I think everyone would love to have financial
freedom. To be able to live how you want to live and not owe anyone
anything would be great. Have you ever thought about what you would
do with the money you make if you didn't owe anything to anyone?
How would your attitude be toward others? God knew that when you
are indebted to someone it can cause division, stress and discord. The
debt is not always money. It can be an apology, time, forgiveness, a
smile, or maybe you owe someone a phone call. God wants you to live
in this life without debt to others. Search your heart and allow God to
reveal to you what, if anything, you may owe to someone. It's time to
pay up and be able to live a life of love to one another!*

You are blessed to be a Blessing!

*My prayer for you today is that you only
owe love to everyone you know.*

July 13

Your scripture for today:

Isaiah 26:12

**Lord, you establish peace for us;
all that we have accomplished you have done for us.**

Observation:

*Take a moment and think of something you accomplished that in the
beginning you might have thought it could never get done. When you
look at it you can testify that it had to be the Lord that helped you get
through it. Everything you have accomplished there was a peace that
came with it. There may have been some obstacles that came but God
gives us His peace when we are doing what He purposed us to do. You
have a knowing in your Spirit that it is right and you are able to do it
with ease and grace. Continue to seek His peace and He will lead you
to accomplish all that He put you here to be, do and have!*

You are blessed to be a Blessing!

*My prayer for you today is that you will have peace
in every plan and goal that you make!*

July 14

Your scripture for today:

Jeremiah 6:16

**Ask where the good way is, and walk in it,
and you will find rest for your souls.**

Observation:

I have heard the saying, 'Don't take advice from anyone that you wouldn't trade places with.' There are many people who love to give their opinion and advice to others. They are very judgmental and like to give advice but won't take it from anyone. You must do things their way or no way! Be very careful who you take advice from. Have you ever felt lost and can't seem to find your way in a situation? You ask for good advice but if it's not what you wanted to hear you go ask someone else. Sometimes what you need to hear is not what you want to hear, but we resist what we need the most. Meditate on any advice you get to make sure it is right for you. Trust your universal guidance system. God knows the right way, the sure way, and the way that is best for you, so that your soul will be at peace.

You are blessed to be a Blessing!

> *My prayer for you today is that you will go to God first and ask for the advice you need. It's found in the Word of God!*

Your scripture for today:

James 3:13

**Who is wise and understanding among you? Let
him show it by his good life, by deeds done in
the humility that comes from wisdom.**

Observation:

*Wisdom is a powerful blessing from God that He gives freely to
those who desire to have it. It doesn't always come with age or with a
college degree. There are many young people who possess wisdom and
knowledge way beyond their years. You ask how they would know to
do the things they do but when God gives you wisdom it's always on
another level. Having wisdom and understanding makes you wise in
everyday deeds and actions, giving insight in business affairs, where
the best deals are and being in the right place at the right time. You
can live your best life now, just seek wisdom and understanding that
only comes from God!*

You are blessed to be a Blessing!

*My prayer for you today is; Thank you Lord that you provide
wisdom to those who ask and want to receive it from you. Give
them wisdom and understanding in every area of their life so
they can live the abundant life that you have in store for them.*

July 16

Your scripture for today:

John 10:10

The thief comes only in order to steal and kill and destroy. I came that they may have and enjoy life, and have it in abundance (to the full, till it overflows).

Observation:

No matter what the enemy has attempted to do. I do not care what others have said about you. It doesn't even matter what trouble you currently find yourself in. In spite of it all, you are blessed. The enemy is out to destroy you and distract you because he knows God has His hand on you and your future is bright. Recognize the tricks of the enemy because there is nothing new. Continue to get closer to God and follow His lead. He is going before you blocking the enemy, knocking out any opposition and making your path straight. So, don't forget how truly blessed you really are. Give God a radical praise of thanksgiving today, a praise that comes out of your mouth. Not just a hand clap or a thought, but a praise where words exit your mouth. He has kept you, and will continue to keep you all the days of your life! So praise Him!

You are blessed to be a Blessing!

My prayer for you today: Thank you God for leading and guiding our path. You are shielding us from all the enemies' tricks and devious tactics. Praise, glory and honor belong to you Lord you are so worthy to be praised!

July 17

Your scripture for today:

2 Thessalonians 2:16-17

May our Lord Jesus Christ himself and God our Father, who loved us and by his grace gave us eternal encouragement and good hope, encourage your hearts and strengthen you in every good deed and word.

Observation:

God's love and encouragement exist outside all relations of time it is not subject to change. It lives on through setbacks, disappointments in life, and even when we are downing ourselves. God's message is given to inspire us with courage, spirit, and confidence to be strong in the Lord and the power of his might! Your good deeds are blessed, your words are blessed, and your finances are blessed! Every good thing that you set your focus on, that is inspired by God and will help others is already blessed! Remember every good deed is inspired by God. Don't hesitate to do it, don't second guess that thought because that second thought is yours not God's. How many times have you been given a thought and you think again only to realize that you should have followed your first mind. Be encouraged because your every move is blessed!

You are blessed to be a Blessing!

My prayer for you today:
Lord thank you that we can be encouraged in everything that we do that is inspired by you! Thank you for all that you lead us to do for the good of your people!

Your scripture for today:

Isaiah 55:12

**You will go out in joy and be led forth in peace; the mountains and hills will burst into song before you, and all the trees of the field
will clap their hands.**

Observation:

Have you ever visualized something in your mind and then seen it happen exactly the way you visualized it? My brother Dan is an amazing artist. I have watched him think of something and transfer it unto a canvas. Think about times that you thought about something and you were able to make it happen. I believe that God has given all of us the ability to create the things that will fulfill His purpose on the earth. All the inventors, artist, entrepreneurs, builders, and writers had to first get that vision than step out on faith to bring it to reality. So when you have received a vision from God, JOY and PEACE will be with you. Even the hills, mountains and trees will be doing the happy dance for you because it is already done. Keep the faith, be encouraged, be grateful, and move forward to your destiny!

You are blessed to be a Blessing!

My prayer for you today:
Lord help us to be open to the visions that you have purposed for us to bring into existence. Help us to step out on faith and make it happen with ease and grace!

July 19

Your scripture for today:

Job 5:8-9

"But if I were you, I would appeal to God; I would lay my cause before him. He performs wonders that cannot be fathomed, miracles that cannot be counted."

Observation:

I know you have heard about prisoners that petition to appeal the sentence they were given in order to have an earlier release. It's a formal process that has to go to a board to make the decision. I have also heard when there is no appeal option because the crime was just that bad. Isn't it great to know that you can appeal to God for anything that you are in need of? With God it doesn't matter what was done you still have an open door to repent and be forgiven. His offer for eternal life is always available to you. He is your very present help in times of trouble. He is able to do more than we can even ask or think. Just remember to take it to God, whatever it may be, so that you can experience the miracle working power that He performs every day!

You are blessed to be a Blessing!

My prayer for you today:
Lord thank you that we can always appeal to you to
be in your good grace and receive eternal life!

July 20

Your scripture for today:

Psalm 36:7-9

How exquisite your love, O God! How eager we are to run under your wings, to eat our fill at the banquet you spread as you fill our tankards with Eden spring water. You're a fountain of cascading light, and you open our eyes to light.

Observation:

God's love for you is better than anything you can imagine! His thoughts are not our thoughts and his ways are totally different than what we can conceive. So the way He loves us is deeper than we would be able to comprehend. In most cases our love is conditional. It's based on how someone makes you feel or what they have done for you lately. But God's love is unconditional and not based on emotions or actions. No matter what is going on around you, God is always there to cover you with His love and protect you from all hurt, harm or danger. He is your provider and will always give you what you need. As you meditate on His goodness you will be filled with the light of love, peace, joy and gratitude! His light will shine through you so others can see. You bring the light into the dark places of this world because God is in you!

You are blessed to be a Blessing!

My prayer for you today:
God thank you for your unconditional love for us!

Your scripture for today:

Joel 2:25-26

I will repay you for the years the locusts have eaten the great locust and the young locust, the other locust and locust swarm my great army that I sent among you. You will have plenty to eat, until you are full, and you will praise the name of the Lord your God, who has worked wonders for you: never again will my people be shamed.

Observation:

God wants to restore you! He is in the restoration business, so what you need, He's got it! God is going to repay back to you double for your trouble, so give glory to God. Think of anything you can give thanks for and with that attitude of gratitude begin to give God thanks. No matter how small it may seem God can bless that! Those who are thankful are fruitful and those who are thankless are fruitless. Let's begin each day with thanksgiving in our hearts and praise in our mouths!

You are blessed to be a Blessing!

My prayer for you today:
Lord help us to be thankful at all times and keep believing that you will restore all that we have lost. Thank you for supplying our every need and giving us double for our trouble.

Your scripture for today:

Proverbs 3:1-2

**My children, do not forget my teaching, but keep my commands
in your heart, for they will prolong your life many years
and bring you peace and prosperity.**

Observation:

*There are times in our lives when we have to be reminded of the
teachings of wisdom that our mentors, parents and the word of God
tell us. They are teachings that are for our goodwill to help us live a
life of prosperity and peace. It's easy to get off track because of the
negative and pessimistic environment that we may be surrounded by.
I have learned that we have to remind ourselves of the good that God
has for us every minute, every hour, and every day! Don't dwell on
the circumstances, but shift your focus to what you really want to see
manifest in your life! Peace & Prosperity are your birthright!*

You are blessed to be a Blessing!

*My prayer for you today:Thank you Lord for the peace and
prosperity that you have already provided for each of your children!*

July 23

Your scripture for today:

Proverbs 16:3

**Commit to the Lord whatever you do,
and your plans will succeed.**

Observation:

Making plans for an awesome future? Make sure to commit them to God. Proverbs 16:7 says; 'When a man's ways are pleasing to the Lord, he makes even his enemies live at peace with him.' When your plans are blessed by God you will have favor and grace to make them succeed. You will have peace and supernatural breakthroughs that will come from your heavenly Father! So as you write your vision, take time out of your busy schedule to get with God so that your ways will be pleasing to Him.

You are blessed to be a Blessing!

*My prayer for you today:
Lord as we make our plans be a part of them so
that your purpose will prevail in our lives!*

July 24

Your scripture for today:

Psalm 31:19

**How abundant are the good things that you have
stored up for those who fear you that you bestow in
the sight of all, on those who take refuge in you.**

Observation:

*I love to go shopping for gifts. It's a fun time to buy things for those you
love. When it's holiday season I usually try to complete my shopping a
couple of months ahead to avoid the shopping frenzy. However, I have
to organize where I will store the gifts so that the surprise won't be
ruined. God has so many great gifts stored up and waiting to present
to you. He wants to make sure you're ready to receive them and you
will have them. All the good things that God has for you are coming
your way for all to see. He has abundant blessings stored up for all who
diligently seek Him and are ready to receive them. Prepare your mind
to receive the goodness of the Lord. Meditate on His word, be devoted
to prayer, honor God in all that you do and seek His protection. Get
ready and expect to receive all the goodness of the Lord.*

You are blessed to be a Blessing!

My prayer for you today:
Lord help us to be ready to receive every gift that
you have stored up with our names on them!

Your scripture for today:

Proverbs 23:7

For as he thinks in his heart, so is he.

Observation:

Do you realize that it doesn't matter what others think of you? It's all about what you think about yourself that matters. If you think you can; you can. If you think you can't; you won't. Anything you can conceive and believe in your heart you will achieve in your life. Our lives today are the direct result of our past and present thoughts, feelings, words, emotions, and desires. You have the power to change anything in your life by merely changing your thoughts. Thank God for your blessings, think positive things about your future, and create the life you truly desire to live!

You are blessed to be a Blessing!

My prayer for you today:
Thank you God for giving us the ability to think good thoughts and live our best life here on earth.

July 26

Your scripture for today:

Galatians 5:22-23

But the fruit of the Spirit is love, joy, peace, patience, kindness, goodness, faithfulness, gentleness and self-control. Against such things there is no law.

Observation:

'Since we live by the Spirit, let us keep in step with the Spirit.' (Galatians 5:25) We can be in step with the Spirit by practicing and living by the fruit of Spirit listed. They will build your character and establish your reputation as a person that is a true child of God. When you decide to live your life by the fruit of the Spirit there is no time to hate on someone else because you have love, joy and peace in your heart. There's no time for anger because you are patient, kind and gentle. Others can count on you because you are faithful. You are never out of control because you have self-control! There is no law that will stand against the fruit of Spirit!

You are blessed to be a Blessing!

My prayer for you today:
Lord I believe that you have established my footsteps and given us the fruit of the spirit to keep in steps with you! Continue to bless us so that we are able to be faithful and self-controlled.

July 27

Your scripture for today:

Psalm 63:3-4

**Because your love is better than life, my lips will
glorify you. I will praise you as long as I live,
and in your name I will lift up my hands.**

Observation:

*Have you ever had a child come to you and want to be picked up? They
will lift their arms and hands up to you which indicates they want to be
picked up. When you pick them up they automatically know to wrap
their legs around you to hold on. At that point no matter what that
child might have done you hold them, love them, and support them
with your loving arms. God loves us unconditionally, through our
faults, our sins, and even when we forget to give Him the honor that
he deserves. When you begin to think about all that He has done for
you, what He has blessed you with, how He made a way out of no way,
how he healed you or your loved one, and provided for you, all you
can do is lift your hands and glorify His name. Let nothing separate
you from the Love of God!*

You are blessed to be a Blessing!

My prayer for you today:
*Lord continue to love us to life. Thanks you for your loving
kindness. We will praise you all the days of our lives!*

July 28

Your scripture for today:

Zechariah 9:16-17

On that day the Lord their God will save them,
as the flock of his people; for like the jewels of a crown
they shall shine on his land.
For how great is his goodness, and how great his beauty!

Observation:

I was watching the Miss Universe pageant and was amazed at the elaborate costumes each contestant wore to represent their country. They were colorful, intricate, and very creative. You could tell each young lady was so proud to be there and eager to win and be crowned the winner! They were all winners already to be there representing their country because they had to have won the local competitions to be in this one. You may think this is just a beauty pageant but for these women it was a battle and they fought to get to this point. Whatever battle you are facing, God has already fought it for you and will make sure that you are victorious! No weapon formed against you will prosper because you already have the victory! Lean on and rely on the goodness of God, knowing that He sees you, and wants you to shine bright like a diamond! Don't lean on your own understanding, trust Him and know that you are the jewels in Gods crown.

You are blessed to be a Blessing!

My prayer for you today:
Thank you Lord for always fighting our battles and giving us the victory in whatever battle we find ourselves in.

July 29

Your scripture for today:

Psalm 55:22

**Cast your burden on the Lord, and he will sustain you;
he will never permit the righteous to be moved.**

Observation:

God will give you what you need to sustain you. Just like he commanded the Ravens to supply food for Elijah in 1 Kings 17, he will also do the same thing for you. When you are feeling like everything is coming against you and the trials are taking over, you have to release all of it and let it go! God wants you to give it all to Him. He is able to handle it. He wants you to be at peace! You don't have to know how it's going to get done. Your job is to cast your cares, release your fears, believe that God's got your back, and trust the process. Peace is with you!

You are blessed to be a Blessing!

My prayer for you today:
God thank you for providing our every need! You are in control of everything and can command even the Ravens to provide for us. You are so good and we praise you!

July 30

Your scripture for today:

Nehemiah 10:39

...We will not neglect the house of our God.

Observation:

When I was growing up, going to church was always something we did. It was not even a question whether we were going or not and it wasn't just on Sunday. There was Bible Study on Wednesday, Choir rehearsal on Tuesday, and if you were in any other groups you might be there every day of week. As a child you get used to doing whatever your parents do. When you get to the teenage years you might wonder why they would go so often. But, I always thought it was great to be able to gather together at Church and worship God in the sanctuary! It's like a filling station to get powered up in the Spirit. When you get involved in some of the volunteer ministries at your church, your experience will be even better! But we also have to look at the fact that we are the temple of God because he lives in us! Make sure to take care of your body every day. Begin to eat healthy and exercise. Do things that are good for you and bring you joy! Remind yourself to be good to yourself! Do not neglect the church house or your house!

You are blessed to be a Blessing!

My prayer for you today:
Lord God help us to take care of your house and our house!

Your scripture for today:

Romans 1:17

**The good news shows how God makes people right
with himself. From beginning to end, becoming right
with God depends on a person's faith. It is written,
"Those who are right with God will live by faith."**

Observation:

*Don't you love to hear good news? We are always hearing negative
news on the popular news shows. They say that the majority of people
want to hear the bad news instead of the good. Well I am not one of
those people. Good news gives positive hope for the future which helps
to build your faith. Whatever God's purpose is for your life it is going
to require you to have faith to accomplish it. God has given each of
us the measure of faith that we need to pursue the purpose that we
are here for. As we walk through this life there will be many steps and
with every step faith is required. As Dr. Martin Luther King said; "You
don't have to see the whole staircase just take the first step and God
will reveal the next, and the next, and the next!"*

You are blessed to be a Blessing!

*My prayer for you today:
I pray that your faith will increase so that you accomplish
everything God put you here to accomplish!*

AUGUST

August 1

Your scripture for today:

Proverbs 24:3-4

**By wisdom a house is built, and through understanding
it is established; through knowledge its rooms
are filled with rare and beautiful treasures.**

Observation:

*When you take the time to ask God for wisdom you also must ask
for wisdom's two best friends understanding and knowledge! With
the 3 working together in your life there is nothing you can't do.
God's wisdom builds you up on the inside, understanding his word
establishes you and gives a strong foundation, then knowledge lavishes
you with blessings until they overflow onto others.*

You are blessed to be a Blessing!

My prayer for you today:
*Thank you God for your wisdom, knowledge and understanding.
You give us all that we need to succeed and transform our lives into
the beautiful image that you ordained for us! Thank you God!*

Your scripture for today:

Proverbs 11:24-25

**One person gives freely, yet gains even more;
another withholds unduly, but comes to poverty. A generous
person will prosper; whoever refreshes others will be refreshed.**

Observation:

*Give and it will be given back to you, pressed down shaken together
and running over! That's how God blesses those who understand they
are blessed to be a blessing! Be a giver and you will always have more
than enough. Give your time, give a smile, give a kind word, and
give out of the abundance of your heart. A closed hand can't expect
anything from God. Open up your hand and God will fill it!*

You are blessed to be a Blessing!

My prayer for you today:
*God you bless those who you know you can get the blessing through.
Help us to be the vessel that you can use to bless your people!*

August 3

Your scripture for today:

1 Corinthians 2:12

**Now we have received not the spirit of the world,
but the Spirit who is from God, that we might
understand the things freely given us by God.**

Observation:

*When you understand that God has given you His spirit to be able
to have His wisdom and insight in all things, you will know that
everything you need to succeed is within you. That's why it's so
important to meditate and spend quiet time with God. Listen for His
voice within you telling you what your next move should be. Turn off
the noise that comes from all directions. Clear your mind of all worry,
fear, and doubt so that you can have room to hear the word of faith,
favor, and victory for your life!*

You are blessed to be a Blessing!

*My prayer for you today:
Lord help us to live by our Spirit that you gave
us to lead and guide us in this life!*

August 4

Your scripture for today:

Philippians 1:18-19

**...Yes, I will continue to rejoice, for I know that through
your prayers and the help given by the Spirit of Jesus Christ,
what has happened to me will turn out for my deliverance.**

Observation:

*When you reflect on the things that have come against you in the pass
you can see that there was always a lesson in it. Hind sight is always
20/20. But while you are in the midst of it, it's hard to see through the
storm. Just continue to rejoice, and don't be afraid to ask for prayer.
The prayers of a righteous man/woman avails and we all stand in need
of prayer. Remember that this too shall pass, seek God continually
because he will deliver you out of whatever situation it is!*

You are blessed to be a Blessing!

*My prayer for you today is that you make your home the one
place where love, peace and joy will overflow! Thank God that
we can live in peace and allow prayer to be in our house!*

August 5

Your scripture for today:

Psalms 111:10

**The fear of the Lord is the beginning of wisdom;
all those who practice it have a good understanding.
His praise endures forever!**

Observation:

*Wisdom starts by knowing and understanding that God created
you, breathed life into you, and put you here for His purpose! As you
acknowledge that truth you will begin to see all that God has for you.
Your eyes will be opened to the supernatural wisdom that only He gives
to those who love him and are called according to His purpose. Give
Him the praise and honor that is due and you will see the goodness
that only God can give!*

You are blessed to be a Blessing!

> *My prayer for you today is that you will reverence
> the Lord and get the wisdom that only He can give.
> Praise you Lord for your awesome wisdom!*

Your scripture for today:

Psalms 52:8

**But as for me, I am like a green olive tree in the house of
God; I trust in the loving kindness of God forever and ever.**

Observation:

*When others have turned away from God and it might even seem like
they are succeeding in their own power. Stay rooted and planted in the
house of God and following His will and plan for your life. Trust in His
unfailing love for you because you are His child and He will not guide
you down a path of destruction. Trust and know that your best is yet
to come. It will be rooted and grounded in love! It will not fail because
when God does it, it will exceed anything you could ask or think!*

You are blessed to be a Blessing!

*My prayer for you today is that you will stay rooted and ground
in the Lord. Keep your faith no matter what's going on around
you! God will bless you and keep you, just keep the faith!*

August 7

Your scripture for today:

2 Corinthians 12:9

**But he said to me, "My grace is sufficient for you,
for my power is made perfect in weakness."**

Observation:

*I can remember a time when the girls were playing outside and I heard
a cry for help. My daughter had fallen and scrapped her knee. She was
crying and of course the sight of blood made her think it was worse
than it was. But she knew to call for help because she needed that extra
strength to get up and she wanted to be rescued. Have you ever just
stopped in the middle of the madness and cried out to God for help. He
is right here waiting for your request. We try to do everything in our
own power and have supernatural power ready to assist us. Surrender
your will in the situation, count to three, and say GOD I NEED YOUR
HELP! The key to this is to stop and listen for His direction.*

You are blessed to be a Blessing!

*My prayer for you today is that you will cry out to
God for the help that you need at any time because
he will always be there to rescue you!*

August 8

Your scripture for today:

Proverbs 13:12

**Hope deferred makes the heart sick, but when
the desire is fulfilled, it is a tree of life.**

Observation:

*When someone gets depressed it's easy to see that their hope is gone.
The issues and problems have taken over and they can't see any way
of escape. When your heart is sick with depression or discouragement,
there is no evidence of hope for the future. But this is not what God
wants for us because he sent His son to give us life and life more
abundantly. If you don't have hope you can't have faith. Hope is key
ingredient to have faith. Remember faith is the evidence of things hoped
for. Therefore we need to always have hope! Reverend Jesse Jackson's
motto is "Keep hope alive" and I believe that you must continue to hope
for new things in your life. You must dream bigger, dream beyond your
surroundings and circumstances. Allow your imagination to reach
new heights and trust that God will bring it to pass.*

You are blessed to be a Blessing!

*My prayer for you today is that you keep hope alive in your
life and live the abundant life that God has in store for you!*

August 9

Your scripture for today:

2 Thessalonians 2:16-17

**May our Lord Jesus Christ himself and God our
Father, who loved us and by his grace gave us eternal
encouragement and good hope, encourage your hearts
and strengthen you in every good deed and word.**

Observation:

*God's love and encouragement for us never die, they live on through
setbacks, disappointments, and even times when we are down on
ourselves. God's message is be encouraged and have good hope be
strong in the Lord and the power of his might! The greater one lives
within you so don't be moved by things that may be coming against
you! You are a child of the highest God who has protected you before
and will continue to do it! So be encouraged!*

You are blessed to be a Blessing!

> My prayer for you today is that you will be encouraged
> through all test, trials, and setbacks and know
> that any setback is a set up for a comeback!

Your scripture for today:

1 Peter 3:8-9

Finally, all of you live in harmony with one another; be sympathetic, and humble. Do not repay evil with evil or insult with insult, but with blessing, because to this you were called so that you may inherit a blessing.

Observation:

Living a life of harmony is like a peaceful melody. There are many different pitches and quality of sounds but when it is in harmony there is a blending of simultaneous sounds and it is pleasant to the ear. I enjoy listening to singing groups that harmonize well. It's amazing how they sound so great together. It's the same way we can be when we live in harmony with our fellow man. There doesn't have to be strife or drama in our lives because we can choose to live in peace, love and joy. That's how God wants us to live in this life with one another.

You are blessed to be a Blessing!

My prayer for you today is that you live together in peace and harmony with your neighbors, co-workers, family and friends!

August 11

Your scripture for today:

2 Corinthians 9:12

**This service that you perform is not only supplying
the needs of God's people but is also overflowing
in many expressions of thanks to God.**

Observation:

*What service are you called to do? You might not have ever thought
about the fact that what you do is helping so many others because you
just see it as a job. It doesn't matter what it might be if you are helping
someone it is a service and it is what you are called to do at this time.
Don't play it down because it's not your dream position. It might even
be behind the scenes but God sees all things and will bless you because
of your faithfulness. Realize that what you do helps others to see God.
Whatever service you are called to do it is important and supplies a
need of God's people. You are anointed to do it and therefore will cause
others to thank God for you! God is hearing your name a lot so your
blessings are always coming!*

You are blessed to be a Blessing!

*My prayer for you is that you will understand how
important you are in the kingdom of God! Your service is
important and you are a valuable piece to the puzzle!*

Your scripture for today:

James 2:17-18

In the same way, faith by itself, if it is not accompanied by action, is dead. But someone will say, "You have faith; I have deeds." Show me your faith without deeds, and I will show you my faith by what I do.

Observation:

God wants us to have strong faith but how can we say we have faith if we don't do the things He told us to do with the faith. You have heard the saying, 'put your money where your mouth is?' Well this scripture is saying put action where your faith is! There are times that God makes it so clear what we need to do and we don't do it. Don't let fear stop you in your tracks because that is exactly what it will do if you let it over take you. God wants you to have strong faith not strong fear! Show your faith by acting on what God has told you to do as soon as He tells you to do it. There is no need to wait or procrastinate. He has already provided the vision and the provision. All that is required is your action!

You are blessed to be a Blessing!

My prayer for you today is that you will put action to your faith and accomplish all that God has for you!

August 13

Your scripture for today:

Psalm 89:15

**Blessed are those who have learned to acclaim you,
who walk in the light of your presence, O Lord.**

Observation:

To acclaim our Lord is to declare Him ruler, winner by enthusiastic approval. We need to put God first in our lives and acknowledge the fact that he wants to be the Lord of our lives. There is nothing that we are striving for or want in our lives that He is not able to bring to pass. Realize that He wants to be in everything we do and when we allow Him in we are acclaiming Him. For without God's love, God's mercy and grace, nothing we consider important would be possible. So acclaim Him today and every day!

You are blessed to be a Blessing!

> *My prayer for you today is that you will walk in
> the light of God's presence every day!*

Your scripture for today:

Proverbs 23:23

Buy the truth and sell it not; not only that, but also get discernment *and* judgment, instruction and understanding.

Observation:

Become a student of the book of truth, wisdom and knowledge. The Bible! Buy study tools that can help you understand the word of God. Listen to great teachers of the word to get discernment. There are so many stories that can apply to your life now and quite a few examples of Gods people being victorious. Instructions on everything you can imagine, along with an entire book of wisdom in Proverbs. Buy whatever version that's easy for you to understand and read. It's all for you, to give you everything you need!

You are blessed to be a Blessing!

My prayer for you today is that you become student of the book of knowledge and read to show yourself approved!

August 15

Your scripture for today:

1 Peter 4:10-11

Each one should serve others, faithfully administering God's grace in its various forms. If anyone speaks, he should do it as one speaking the very words of God. If anyone serves, he should do it with the strength God provides, so that in all things God may be praised through Jesus Christ. To him be the glory and the power forever and ever. Amen.

Observation:

God gives us each gifts that we can use to serve others. Yours may be different than mine but they are designed to administer God's grace to others. We must know that our purpose in all that we do is to glorify God. So as we serve others, speak to others and work for others they are able to see God in us! Don't be afraid to call on God's strength when you find yourself becoming weak in the process. Build up your strength and encourage yourself to continue to be the best. Be faithful in your service to others and God will be faithful to you. You will have favor, grace and mercy available to you and the power to get it done!

You are blessed to be a Blessing!

My prayer for you today is that you will continue to work with the power of God that's available to you at all times!

August 16

Your scripture for today:

2 Peter 1:3

**His divine power has given us everything we need
for life and godliness through our knowledge of him
who called us by his own glory and goodness.**

Observation:

*In this life it seems like it's all about who you know in order to get the
big breaks. It's great to know the right people to help you get a job or
give you a discount on things. But it is more powerful to know the
King of Kings and Lord of Lords! It doesn't matter who you know in
the natural realm because God has already walked out your footsteps
and designed a life of victory, favor and grace that you deserve. So get
to know Almighty God so that you can be ushered into the VIP section
in this life and the life to come!*

You are blessed to be a Blessing!

*My prayer for you today is that you will get to know the real King
of Kings so you can live a life of victory that he has in store for you!*

August 17

Your scripture for today:

Psalm 36:7-9

**How priceless is your unfailing love! Both high and low
among men find refuge in the shadow of your wings.
They feast on the abundance of your house; you give
them drink from your river of delights. For with you
is the fountain of life; in your light we see light.**

Observation:

*There is no one else that you can go to for unfailing love, where you
can find refuge, get abundance, a fountain of life and light all in one
except God. He is our all in all. Everything we need is found in Him.
You can search for all eternity long and find there is none like our God.
This is not something money can buy. It's all about your desire to be
close to your creator and father God. He is the fountain of life and
refuge. The currency that gets Gods attention is your faith and belief
in him. Believe in Him, give Him your heart, and abundance will be
in your house!*

You are blessed to be a Blessing!

*My prayer for you today is that you will give your whole heart to
God and watch Him bless you with the true riches that you deserve.*

August 18

Your scripture for today:

Psalm 27:13-14

I would have lost heart, unless I had believed that I would see the goodness of the Lord in the land of the living. Wait on the Lord; be of good courage, and He will strengthen your heart, wait, I say, on the Lord!

Observation:

We have to stay encouraged and not lose heart. The dreams and desires God has placed in us will come to past! Believe that God placed that dream in your heart therefore he will help you make it happen. We usually have a problem with the wait on the Lord part. We usually decide to help God out while we wait, just in case He needs our help to figure out how and when the dream needs to be completed. Remember God knows when we are ready to receive that blessing! His timing is always best. Trust and believe and you will have the goodness of the Lord in the land of the living!

You are blessed to be a Blessing!

My prayer for you today is that you can believe that God will bring your dreams and desires into existence! Trust in His timing!

August 19

Your scripture for today:

Proverbs 16:2-3

**All a man's ways seem innocent to him, but motives
are weighed by the Lord. Commit to the Lord
whatever you do, and your plans will succeed.**

Observation:

*We must remember that God knows what we are thinking and the
reason we do what we do! Whether it's to be seen by others or to brag
about what we have done. He knows the reason why you are doing
it. Keep your motives and your heart pure. When you do things for
others it doesn't matter if anyone else knows about it. God's blessings
and favor on your life will be apparent to others. Commit your plans
to God he is excited and ready to make your plans successful!*

You are blessed to be a Blessing!

*My prayer for you today is that you will examine your reason
for doing what you do and commit your ways to the Lord!*

Your scripture for today:

Psalm 26:2-3

**Test me, O Lord, and try me, examine my heart
and my mind; for your love is ever before me,
and I walk continually in your truth.**

Observation:

*God knows what is in your heart and what you are thinking about.
It is a confident person who can boldly say to God test me! Having a
pure heart and thinking good thoughts is what God wants for us. It
says in Philippians 4:7-8 and the peace of God, which transcends all
understanding, will guard your hearts and your minds in Christ Jesus.
Finally, brother, whatever is true, whatever is noble, whatever is right,
whatever is pure, whatever is lovely, whatever is admirable if anything
is excellent or praiseworthy think about such things.*

You are blessed to be a Blessing!

*My prayer for you today is that you will think about what
you have been thinking about and understand that your
thoughts are creating your future. Lord help us to think
the thoughts that you want us to think at all times!*

August 21

Your scripture for today:

2 Corinthians 8:11-12

**Now finish the work, so that your eager willingness to do it may
be matched by your completion of it, according to your means.
For if the willingness is there, the gift is acceptable according
to what one has, not according to what he does not have.**

Observation:

*Have you ever had to totally rely on God to bring you the provisions
you need to finish the work? I have experienced this time and time
again because of running my own business. There are times when
things look like it's not going to happen. The production we need to
continue the work is not there and it's tempting to begin to doubt
that it's going to happen. But God blesses the motive and purpose of
what you do. He knows your heart and gives you the creative ideas,
ability, and gifts according to your willingness to do it. He then adds
His supernatural power with your natural to make sure it is blessed!
When God is in it don't stop, keep pushing forward and your dreams
will come to pass!*

You are blessed to be a Blessing!

> *My prayer for you today is that you keep going and believe
> that God will finish the work that he started in you!*

Your scripture for today:

2 Corinthians 5:5

Now it is God who has made us for this very purpose and has given us the Spirit as a deposit, guaranteeing what is to come.

Observation:

When Jesus left to be with the Father God he left us with the Holy Spirit. He even said that we would do even greater works than he did because of it! So he made a deposit in us just like what we make in our bank accounts. The difference is the Holy Spirit gives us power that money cannot buy. We are powerful and able to be, do and have anything our heart desires that is within God's will. So run with God's Spirit that is within you it is powerful!

You are blessed to be a Blessing!

My prayer for you today is that you realize the deposit that God made in you was more powerful than money can buy. Thank God for your powerful investment in us!

August 23

Your scripture for today:

Ecclesiastes 5:18-20

Then I realized that it is good and proper for a man to eat and drink, and to find satisfaction in his toilsome labor under the sun during the few days of life God has given him for this is his lot. Moreover, when God gives any man wealth and possessions, and enables him to enjoy them, to accept his lot and be happy in his work~ this is a gift of God. He seldom reflects on the days of his life, because God keeps him occupied with gladness of heart.

Observation:

This is how God wants us to be! Enjoying what we do every day, having wealth and full of joy. You may be doing a job that you dislike right now, but begin to declare that you are happy no matter what the circumstances may be. Receive the gift of joy from God and decide to be happy and not worrying about the day. Make a choice to have gladness in your heart. When things get crazy just remind yourself that God gave you the gift of joy so don't give it away or allow someone or something to steal it!

You are blessed to be a Blessing!

My prayer for you today:
Lord give us your joy every day so that we can enjoy the fruits of our labor and as we obtain wealth and prosperity our house will be happy, loving, and full of the love of God!

August 24

Your scripture for today:

Isaiah 40:31

**Those who hope in the Lord will renew their strength.
They will soar on wings like eagles; they will run and
not grow weary, they will walk and not faint.**

Observation:

*Have you ever been tired of being tired? There are times when we just
go, go, and go, doing everything for everybody. You have given until
you can't give any more. This is the time when you are in need of the
Lord's energy boost. Sounds like a drink you buy in the store like
Red Bull! However, this is so much better because it renews you with
the power of God. Stop for God's energy boost and allow him to be
your strength. He wants you to be strong and not weak. As it says in
Galatians 6:9 Let us not become weary in doing good, for at the proper
time we will reap a harvest if we do not give up.*

You are blessed to be a Blessing!

My prayer for you today:
*Lord thank you for your strength when we are weak. Take
us to new levels in you and help us to not become weary and
faint! You will take us through all the trials and tribulations
we may face so thank you because the best is yet to come!*

August 25

Your scripture for today:

Proverbs 10:22

**The blessings of the Lord bring wealth,
and he adds no trouble to it.**

Observation:

It's so encouraging to know that as God blesses us we will be wealthy in so many ways. Having joy, happiness, laughter, health, family, and friends is a part of having wealth. As we open our heart to receive the blessings, and mature in our ability to handle the wealth in our lives, God is able to give us more. If we can't handle a little wealth why would God give us more? Be faithful with the little and increase will come. Remember God says he wants us to prosper and be in health even as our soul prospers. So get ready to receive your blessings!

You are blessed to be a Blessing!

My prayer for you today is:
You have the victory so be encouraged that God will give you peace and not drama, blesses and not curses, wealth and not poverty. Thank you God you are so good to your children!

Your scripture for today:

Isaiah 26:3-4

You will keep in perfect peace him whose mind is steadfast, because he trusts in you. Trust in the Lord forever, for the Lord, the Lord is the Rock eternal.

Observation:

This is a song of praise to the Lord for keeping our minds in perfect peace. But we have a part to play in it. We must focus on him instead of our problem. We must train ourselves to think positive thoughts because as you think in your hearts, so are you. There is a peace that comes when we do. Worry is negative meditation, but when we magnify our God and seek his face, taking all the burdens and giving them to him our meditation is peaceful. Trust that he will take care of your problems because he cares about you. We can be in perfect peace just trust in God!

You are blessed to be a Blessing!

My prayer for you today:
Bless our minds Lord so that we are able
to have your peace at all times!

Your scripture for today:

2 Thessalonians 2:16-17

**May our Lord Jesus Christ himself and God our
Father, who loved us and by his grace gave us eternal
encouragement and good hope, encourage your hearts
and strengthen you in every good deed and word.**

Observation:

*God's love and encouragement for us never dies, it lives on through
setbacks, disappointments in life, and even when we are downing
ourselves. God's message is be encouraged and have good hope be
strong in the Lord and the power of his might! When you do good deeds
God is pleased. When you speak encouraging words to others, God is
pleased. Just don't forget to do good things for yourself and encourage
yourself by speaking positive affirmations every day. Live your life by
giving your life and you will recognize that you are a vessel that God
can use here on earth. Be encouraged!*

You are blessed to be a Blessing!

My prayer for you today:
Live to give! Thank God for your encouragement and good hope!

August 28

Your scripture for today:

Psalm 30:4-5

Sing to the Lord, you saints of his; praise his holy names. For his anger last only a moment, but his favor lasts a lifetime; weeping may remain for a night, but rejoicing comes in the morning.

Observation:

We may have setbacks and things in our past that rob us of our joy. Just keep in mind that as long as we don't continue to look back, we can move forward with God's everlasting favor. It's ok to cry and let it out just put a time limit on those tears because when the tears dry up you can look for the lesson in that obstacle. With every new morning comes a new opportunity to have joy, peace, love, and blessings. You will be stronger because you understand that trouble doesn't last always. So be encouraged, no matter what's going on!

You are blessed to be a Blessing!

> *My prayer for you today is that you will understand that things come to pass and not to stay. Look to the future because it is brighter then you realize!*

August 29

Your scripture for today:

1 Peter 5:5-6

Young men, in the same way be submissive to those who are older. All of you clothe yourselves with humility toward one another, because, "God opposes the proud but gives grace to the humble." Humble yourselves, therefore, under God's mighty hand, that he may lift you up in due time.

Observation:

Being humble doesn't mean to be less than or to neglect yourself. It means to give honor where honor is due understanding that everything you have you have because of God's grace, mercy and unmerited favor on your life. Put on humility like you are putting on a jacket. It's a choice! You can choose to be prideful and arrogant, or be humble and get all the blessings that God has in store for you.

You are blessed to be a Blessing!

My prayer for you today:
Thank you God for your grace. Continue to give grace and mercy to all those who are humble and give you all the honor and praise.

Your scripture for today:

Hebrews 10:23-24

**Let us hold unswervingly to the hope we profess, for he
who promised is faithful. And let us consider how we
may spur one another on toward love and good deeds.**

Observation:

*When we know the promises that God has for us we can have hope
and be cheerleaders for others whose hope is fading. As we encourage
others we too will be encouraged. Remember to plant seeds of peace
and love throughout your day! Hold onto the hope that we have in
the Lord. Profess it and declare His goodness everywhere you go. You
will be a shining example and true role model of Gods goodness to His
children. Others may never read the Bible but they will observe you to
see if what they have heard about God is really true.*

You are blessed to be a Blessing!

*My prayer for you today is that you will be a
shining example of the goodness of God!*

August 31

Your scripture for today:

James 5:7-8

Be patient, then brothers, until the Lord's coming. See how the farmer waits for the land to yield its valuable crop and how patient he is for the autumn and spring rains. You too, be patient and stand firm, because the Lord's coming is near.

Observation:

I lived in a rural area in Michigan for my last 2 years of high school and many of the people owned farms. I watched how disciplined they were about seed, time, and harvest. The students would be up earlier to do the cores before coming to school. But it was interesting how they had to wait on the harvest. They had to be patient after planting the seeds and continue to water the seeds that were sown. Have you asked God for anything lately? Be patient! The seed has been planted and the Lord will fulfill it. Stand firm and know that it will happen. Just wait on the Lord and water your seed with thanksgiving and faith while you wait for it to come!

You are blessed to be a Blessing!

> *My prayer for you today is that you will have the patience to wait on the Lord for what you need and want. Keep the faith and speak positive words over the seed you have sown and you will reap a harvest of blessings.*

SEPTEMBER

September 1

Your scripture for today:

2 Thessalonians 1:11-12

With this in mind, we constantly pray for you, that our God may count you worthy of his calling, and that by his power he may fulfill every purpose of yours and every act prompted by your faith. We pray this so that the name of our Lord Jesus may be glorified in you and you in him, according to the grace of our God and the Lord Jesus Christ.

Observation:

God is so impressed by your faith. He is eager to jump in to help when you are showing that you have faith in Him to perform in your life. God wants you to succeed in every area of your life because you are a reflection of him on earth! As he fulfills every purpose and act that you begin, others will want to know more about the God you serve. When you have proclaimed that God is able to supply all your needs according to His riches in glory and you have faith to wait on the Lord, He will make things happen for you! Make sure to take time to thank God for the blessings that he has already given you knowing and believing that the best is yet to come!

You are blessed to be a Blessing!

My prayer for you today is that you will glorify the Lord at all times and His praise will continually be on your lips!

September 2

Your scripture for today:

Jude 1:21

Stay always within the boundaries where God's love can reach and bless you. Wait patiently for the eternal life that our Lord Jesus Christ in his mercy is going to give you.

Observation:

The other day traffic was stopped for no apparent reason that I could see from my vantage point. However, as it began to move I saw that the holdup was for a Mother duck and her ducklings crossing the street. They were walking single file but stayed very close together. I am sure if one had got too far out of line the Mom would make sure they got back to where it should be. We must make sure to stay in line with God at all times. Don't get so far out there that you are no longer under His protective umbrella. Stay within reach of His love and comfort. You don't have to do what everyone else does to get ahead! You are blessed and highly favored! Stay close to God and He will stay close to you!

You are blessed to be a Blessing!

> *My prayer for you today is that you will stay close to God so that He can pour out His blessings on you!*

September 3

Your scripture for today:

John 20:21

**Jesus said to them again, "Peace be with you. As the
Father has sent me, even so I am sending you."**

Observation:

*Have you ever had an assignment delegated to you by your manager?
The manager may be working on a bigger project but needs your help
to get one part of it done that will help complete it. You don't always
know why you are having to do it but know that you must get it done.
You should feel great knowing that your Manager had confidence in
you to give you the responsibility to get it done because it is a direct
reflection on him or her. God has delegated a powerful assignment to
us to spread the good news. He expects us to get it done because as we
do others will see Him in us!*

You are blessed to be a Blessing!

My prayer for you today:
*Go in peace and spread the good news and our God will bless
you and you will be a shining reflection of His peace and love!*

September 4

Your scripture for today:

John 20:25

**So the other disciples told him, "We have seen the Lord."
But he said to them, "Unless I see in his hands the mark of
the nails, and place my finger into the mark of the nails,
and place my hand into his side, I will never believe."**

Observation:

*Have you ever had an idea or thought come to you and you got so
excited about that you thought you would share it with your friends
only to hear them say it won't work or that is silly because they haven't
seen anything like that before? Most people are of the school of thought
that seeing is believing or I will believe it when I see it. That is the same
way that Thomas thought in this scripture. He wouldn't believe that
Jesus had risen until He actually showed up to prove he was alive.
Even after all the miracles the disciples witnessed while Jesus was with
them, Thomas still needed proof! Think about how many times God
has done miraculous things because of your faith. You have seen Jesus
so continue to believe!*

You are blessed to be a Blessing!

> *My prayer for you today is: Please remember all
> that Jesus has done in your life! Just believe that
> he is still with you blessing you every day!*

September 5

Your scripture for today:

Acts 2:17

**"'And in the last days it shall be, God declares,
that I will pour out my Spirit on all flesh,
and your sons and your daughters shall prophesy,
and your young men shall see visions,
and your old men shall dream dreams;**

Observation:

When you hear that your favorite music artist is coming to give a concert you get excited and can't wait to buy the tickets. It's even better when someone blesses you with free tickets. But you run and tell everyone that you are going to the concert with excitement and joyful anticipation. You even get the CD's out and start playing them to catch up on all the songs! Well when the biggest Superstar of all decides to come back I believe that he will make sure His children are taken care of because we already have free tickets to the greatest show that will ever be seen. He will give us the vision to know of His coming and we will be able to rejoice in anticipation of his arrival! We will be able to tell others of His coming so that they can be ready. Be open to receive the visions and dreams that he will pour out and praise the Lord with songs and hymns and spiritual songs!

You are blessed to be a Blessing!

My prayer for you today: I pray that you have accepted the free gift of salvation from the one and only Jesus Christ Superstar!

September 6

Your scripture for today:

Luke 11:9-10

**And I tell you, ask, and it will be given to you; seek,
and you will find; knock, and it will be opened to you.
For everyone who asks receives, and the one who seeks
finds, and to the one who knocks it will be opened.**

Observation:

*My nieces and nephews were over to my house one day and they
decided to play a game of hide and go seek. One person would be the
seeker and all the others would try to get a great hiding spot so they
wouldn't be found. The consequences of being found would mean they
were out of the game. We need to be the seeker when it comes to God!
The difference is that God is not hiding from you! He is right out in
the open waiting for you to find Him. He is not worried about being
out the game because He created the game. He will open all the doors
that you need in order to make sure you are abundantly blessed! Seek
Him, seek Him and you will find all that you need!*

You are blessed to be a Blessing!

My prayer for you today:
*Thank you Lord for always being available to those who are
looking for you! Give them all that they need and want!*

September 7

Your scripture for today:

Philippians 1:6

Being confident of this, that he who began a good work in you will carry it on to completion until the day of Christ Jesus.

Observation:

If you have ever had your home remodeled you know how uncomfortable, inconvenient, noisy, dusty, and upside down everything is. But when the project is finished you are amazed at the work and how beautiful it is. Well, God has started a good work in us and he is going to finish it. He is not like man who starts things then changes his mind because of difficult times, or money looks funny, or the weather isn't perfect. No, God started it, he is finishing it, just allow him to complete the project he started and you will be amazed by his awesome work in you!

You are blessed to be a Blessing!

My prayer for you today is that you will allow God to complete the work He began in you!

September 8

Your scripture for today:

Acts 8:4

Those who had been scattered preached the word wherever they went.

Observation:

When you are confident in the Lord and know how the word has ministered to you in your life you will tell others about it. In this scripture Phillip was telling everyone he met about the goodness of God. People were getting healed and cleansed of evil spirits as he told the good news of God. Remember that you are able to bloom where you are planted. You can reach so many people at your job, while you shop, at the beauty salon or barber shop. You have the light so shine it by speaking and giving your testimony of how good God has been to you! Did He heal you or someone you know? Tell about it! Did He provide what you needed right on time? Tell about it! Did He get you out of a difficult situation? Tell about it! Whatever tests that God has brought you through, tell about it! Your test is now your testimony that will save and deliver someone who needed to hear it! Just like the songs say, 'Go tell it on the mountains, over the hills and everywhere!'

You are blessed to be a Blessing!

My prayer for you today is that you will tell everyone you know and those you don't know of the goodness of God!

September 9

Your scripture for today:

Isaiah 46:11

I say: My purpose will stand, and I will do all that I please. From the east I summon a bird of prey; from a far-off land, a man to fulfill my purpose. What I have said, that will I bring about; what I have planned, that will I do.

Observation:

God has a specific purpose that He put you here to accomplish. You are an important part of the big picture that God has already planned. Unless you stay in tuned with the Spirit and get step by step instructions you can get off track of the destination that is intended for you. It's like planning to take a driving trip across country. You check out the map to see which route you want to take. While you are looking over the map you can see the big picture from the start to your final destination. This is just like how God is looking over your life. But, what you can see is only the road a few feet ahead of you. I like to track my progress by checking the road markers that tell you how many miles to the next town. As you go through life you will have good things happen in your life that will let you know that you are on the right track. Just keep moving in the direction that God has for you and you will reach your destination!

You are blessed to be a Blessing!

My prayer for you today is that you have confidence in the directions that God gives to you. His purpose will prevail!

September 10

Your scripture for today:

Ezekiel 36:26-27

I will give you a new heart and put a new spirit in you; I will remove from you your heart of stone and give you a heart of flesh. And I will put my Spirit in you and move you to follow my decrees and be careful to keep my laws.

Observation:

God wants to do a total transformation in you. Everyone is looking for the Extreme Makeover that makes us look better on the outside to be pleasing to the human eyes. But God sees our beauty on the inside and He wants us to be renewed in our Spirit, soul, and our mind! It's hard to look sad and be excited on the inside! It's also difficult to look excited on the outside when your heart is broken. God wants to help you be at peace because He knows that whatever is happening inside will show up on the outside. Therefore just an outward transformation is not enough. The new heart and spirit starts with knowing who you are in Christ and changing how you look at things. Your attitude has to change in order for you to see things in a new and different way! I have heard people say, 'That's just how I am'. But if you want to see something different in your life you can change! What a blessing it is to have a God who cares and wants us to be the best from the inside out!

You are blessed to be a Blessing!

My prayer for you today is that you will be renewed from the inside out every day!

September 11

Your scripture for today:

Malachi 3:16-17

Then those who feared the Lord spoke to one another, and the Lord listened and heard them; so a book of remembrance was written before Him for those who fear the Lord and who meditate on His name. "They shall be mine," says the Lord of hosts, "On the day that I make them my jewels, and I will spare them as a man spares his own son who serves him."

Observation:

Nowadays mostly everyone takes pictures with their smartphones! They store them in their phone until they put them on Facebook, Instagram, one of the other social network sites. The other day I pulled out our photo albums and had a great time looking through them and laughing at the way we were! It took me back to remember all the good times that were shared with loved ones, friends and family. It is great to know that you are in God's book of remembrance. He is taking a picture of you and adding you to the book every time you do a random act of kindness, followed His lead, and just because you are who you are which is His precious jewel! Isn't it awesome to think that God sees us as His jewels! Just think about what we do with our precious jewels. We protect them, insure them, polish them, look at them with delight, and make sure they are well taken care of so no harm or danger comes to them. So remember as we speak about the goodness of God he is hearing us and taking us out of that safe deposit box to look on us with delight. You are His precious jewel!!!

You are blessed to be a Blessing!

My prayer for you today is that you will understand that God is taking your picture for His heavenly book of remembrance so always be ready to smile!

September 12

Your scripture for today:

Galatians 6:4-5

**Each one should test his own actions. Then he can take
pride in himself, without comparing himself to somebody
else, for each one should carry his own load.**

Observation:

*It's good to be independent and to work to get things that you desire.
Just remember that in all that we do make sure to stay dependent on
God to lead and guide you every step of the way. Be confident in your
ability and don't compare yourself to others. What God has put in you
and placed you here to do cannot be compared to what he has placed
in someone else. We all have a part in God's plan. So stay in your own
lane and run a confident race to the finish line!*

You are blessed to be a Blessing!

*My prayer for you today is that you will stay confident in
your ability to get the job done! You have the power and the
wisdom to be the success you always knew you could be!*

September 13

Your scripture for today:

Psalm 41:1

Blessed is he who has regard for the weak; the Lord delivers him in times of trouble.

Observation:

When we help others who are in need God turns around and helps us. We are extensions of God's hands here on earth. As we are led by His Spirit to do things to help those in need, we are allowing God to use us as vessels. God may drop a thought in us to pray for someone and you don't know why. Or give to someone who looks like they have many things already. We don't know what that person has been praying to God for. We just have to be obedient and do what God places on our hearts to do as soon as we get the urge to do it. Be the vessel that God can use and you will always be blessed!

You are blessed to be a Blessing!

My prayer for you today is that you are opened to the prompting of the Holy Spirit to lead you to that person that has been praying for God's miracle. You are able to help that person in need because God sent you to do it!

Your scripture for today:

Isaiah 54:17

**"No weapon forged against you will prevail, and you
will refute every tongue that accuses you. This is
the heritage of the servants of the Lord, and this is
their vindication from me," declares the Lord.**

Observation:

*As children of God there will be various weapons that will try to
form against us. Untrue words spoken, false accusations, and even
those who become envious of our blessings. That is why I love this
declaration, weapons may form but they will not prosper. You won't
have to do anything because God will reveal the truth in the end. It says
that you will prove to be false or erroneous, every tongue that accuses
you. Not by standing on the roof and declaring with a megaphone that
they are wrongly accusing you, but by your actions and Love. We can
have confidence that God's got our back and we are victors and not
victims.*

You are blessed to be a Blessing!

*My prayer for you today is that your peace will rule your life
and you will see that God is fighting your battles for you!*

September 15

Your scripture for today:

Acts 8:22-23

**"Repent of this wickedness and pray to the Lord in the hope
that he may forgive you for having such a thought in your heart.
For I see that you are full of bitterness and captive to sin."**

Observation:

*You must look at what has caused you to be bitter in your heart! If
it is a person that you are holding on to un-forgiveness, you must
forgive them and let it go! Forgiveness is not for them, it is for you!
As long as you are holding on to whatever wrong you feel was done
to you, you will never move forward in your life. You might feel that
you have moved on and forgiven them, but if you see that person and
your stomach still turns; you're not past it yet! Don't allow a root of
bitterness to cause you to lose the blessings that God has stored up for
you! Remember to repent of un-forgiveness, bitterness, and sin so that
you can move on to all the prosperity that God has waiting for you.*

You are blessed to be a Blessing!

> *My prayer for you today is repent of any bitterness,
> un-forgiveness, or sin that you might have! God is in
> the forgiving business and He will forgive you too!*

September 16

Your scripture for today:

1 Corinthians 14:13

God is not the author of confusion, but of peace.

Observation:

An author is the maker, creator or originator of something. We know that God did not create confusion so let the confusion in any situation remind you that God is not in it. When you are feeling confused and your mind is going in all different directions. Imagine coming to a crossroad and not knowing which direction you should go. I believe that if you stop and ask God for peace, he will lead you out of the confusion and into a place of peace. Many times you just need to get away from it for a minute and stop, clear your head, take some deep breaths and allow God to direct your path!

You are blessed to be a Blessing!

> *My prayer for you today is that you will seek peace that comes from your Father God. He is not starting drama or confusion in your life. Remember the enemy comes to kill, steal and destroy, so seek peace at all times!*

September 17

Your scripture for today:

Psalm 25:4-5

**Show me your ways, O Lord, teach me your paths;
guide me in your truth and teach me, for you are my
God my Savior, and my hope is in you all day long.**

Observation:

Many of us have a navigation system in our cars these days. We put in our final destination and the system speaks the directions to us every few minutes. As long as we stay on course the voice tells us to keep going. If we make a wrong turn the voice says "Recalculating". Well God gave us His Spirit to be our Spiritual guidance system to show us the path that he has put in place for us. It speaks to us through our intuition. It's a still small voice that will let us know which way to go! It also warns us when we are getting off track by giving us a knowing in our spirit that something is not right! Just like the navigation system in your car you can override the instructions and go your own way, you can also do that with your spiritual guidance system. You may have found yourself off track but the Holy Spirit will get you back on track. Be open and willing to follow His path. If you make a wrong turn allow Him to Recalculate and get you back on track! Ask and you will receive the direction you need!

You are blessed to be a Blessing!

*My prayer for you today is that you will allow the
Spiritual Guidance System to direct your path!*

Your scripture for today:

Psalm 122:7-9

May there be peace within your walls and security within your citadels. For the sake of my brothers and friends, I will say, "peace be within you." For the sake of the house of the Lord our God. I will seek your prosperity.

Observation:

We should desire peace, security, and prosperity in our homes, with our friends, family, in our city, on our jobs, and in our world. It's good to know that God wants us to have peace within. When we can say "peace be with you", that is planting a seed of peace in someone else. We want to receive the kind of peace where in the midst of the storm you can still have it, when everything is going wrong you still have it, when the bills are due you still have it, when others slander you, you still have it! Peace that passes all understanding! That's the peace of God!

You are blessed to be a Blessing!

My prayer for you today is that you will have peace in every area of your life! Peace be with you!

Your scripture for today:

Matthew 14:28-31

Lord. if it's you, Peter replied, "tell me to come to you on the water". "Come", He said. Then Peter got down out of the boat, walked on the water and came toward Jesus. But when he saw the wind, he was afraid and, beginning to sink, cried out, "Lord, save me!" Immediately Jesus reached out his hand and caught him. "You of little faith," he said. "Why did you doubt?"

Observation:

How many times do we pray to God for a miracle and when we get it we begin to look around at the wind and start listening to people instead of going back to God who provided the miracle for us. Then because we are relying on earthly guidance only (EGO) we become afraid and begin to sink. We must remember those nights we prayed for that miracle before we got it. Just like Peter we asked and He said come but when we take our eyes off Him that's when we begin to sink. The great thing about God is that he is always there to pull us out. Just have faith and keep your eyes on the prize, keep your focus on Him and you will experience miracles every day!

You are blessed to be a Blessing!

My prayer for you today is that you will not let the EGO run your life! Don't allow doubt to enter in and you will see the Lord's salvation!

September 20

Luke 8:50

Hearing this, Jesus said to Jairus, "Don't be afraid; just believe, and she will be healed."

Observation:

Many times before the miracle God would send an angel or make sure to say "don't be afraid"? He knows that we get fearful when something supernatural is about to occur. But his comfort to us is to; just Believe! We don't have to be in control of everything. Let it go, and let God do it for you. Don't listen to the naysayers around you. Your dream may be bigger than your environment, so go for it, Be Not Afraid; Just Believe!

You are blessed to be a Blessing!

My prayer for you today: Lord please give us the ability to see your miracles happen in our lives without fear! Help us to build up our faith in you and believe that you have everything under control.

September 21

Your scripture for today:

Proverbs 23:7

For as he thinks in his heart, so is he.

Observation:

Do you realize that it doesn't matter what others think of you? It's all about what you think about yourself that matters! If you think you can; you can! If you think you can't; you won't! Anything you can conceive and believe in your heart you will achieve in your life. Our lives today are the direct result of our past and present thoughts, feelings, words, emotions, and desires. You have the power to change anything in your life by merely changing your thoughts. Thank God for your blessings, think positive things about your future, and create the life you truly desire to live!

You are blessed to be a Blessing!

My prayer for you today is that you will think positive, good, loving thoughts about yourself, your friends, your family, your job, and everything that concerns you!

September 22

Your scripture for today:

Psalm 67:9-10

You gave abundant showers, O God; you refreshed your weary inheritance. Your people settled in it, and from your bounty, O God, you provided for the poor.

Observation:

God will always give us what we need and in this case it was rain that his people needed. I never understood how having too much or too little rain can affect you until we moved to Texas. I have seen how the overflow of rain can cause major flooding, even to the point that the water is over the top of some homes. I have seen Semi trucks floating in what was the freeway that had become a river. On the other side of that I have also seen when there is a drought and there hasn't been any rain for months. I have seen wild fires that can take over the land in the extreme heat just from a cigarette being tossed out of a window. In our lives we may have periods of drought and seasons of abundant overflow blessings which are extreme situations. But there are also the times that God sends the refreshing showers to bless us. We must remember that God sees what we need; he wants us to be refreshed, and provide our every need, want, and desire! Just trust him!

You are blessed to be a Blessing!

My prayer for you today is that you will experience the refreshing rain that God has to bless your life with all that you need!

September 23

Your scripture for today:

Isaiah 64:8

Yet, O Lord, you are our Father. We are the clay, you are the potter; we are all the work of your hand.

Observation:

If you ever played with play-doe when you were a kid you might remember that in order to transform it into a shape that you wanted you had to take it and squeeze it, roll it and press it out. Than when it got pliable enough you could make it do just about anything you wanted it to do. Once you made it into what you wanted at that time you could change it into something else by repeating the process. Well God is working on us all the time squeezing us with love, rolling us and pressing us into His image. He is molding us and making us into the beautiful possessions that he wants us to be. As long as we allow Him to lead us He will. Be open, willing, and allow God's Spirit to flow in your life. Just imagine his hands sculpting you in His loving and peaceful way.

You are blessed to be a Blessing!

My prayer for you today is that you will allow God to transform you with his loving hands to mold you and make you into His image!

September 24

Your scripture for today:

James 3:13

**Who is wise and understanding among you? Let
him show it by his good life, by deeds done in
the humility that comes from wisdom.**

Observation:

*What would you consider a good life? Many people would have different
views of this but I think the main factor would be having God in the
center of it all. As children of God we are role models whether we want
to be or not! We can be positive role models or negative role models
based on the path we choose to go down. The world looks at and labels
some athletes, rappers, singers, and actors as role models because they
are in the public eye and have successful careers. However, I believe
that many of them just like us have spent hours praying to God for
wisdom and understanding which has made us wise in our everyday
deeds and actions. God's children are the ones that should be living
the good life. It's time to take back what the enemy has stolen and it
will come through wisdom that comes from God!*

You are blessed to be a Blessing!

*My prayer for you today is that you will be mindful
and wise in your everyday deeds and actions. Do
until others as you would have done onto you!*

September 25

Your scripture for today:

Philippians 1:18-19

...Yes, I will continue to rejoice, for I know that through your prayers and the help given by the Spirit of Jesus Christ, what has happened to me will turn out for my deliverance.

Observation:

When you reflect on the things that have come against you in the pass you can see that there was always a lesson in it. Hind sight is always 20/20. But while you are in the midst of it, it's hard to see through the storm. Just continue to rejoice, and don't be afraid to ask for prayer. The prayers of a righteous man/woman avails and we all stand in need of prayer. Remember that this too shall pass, seek God continually because he will deliver you out of whatever situation it is!

You are blessed to be a Blessing!

My prayer for you today is that you will understand that the Lord will deliver you out of anything that comes against you. He is working behind the scenes to make your crooked places straight!

September 26

Your scripture for today:

Ephesians 3:20

Now to Him who is able to do exceedingly abundantly above all that we ask or think, according to the power that works in us, to Him be glory...

Observation:

God is not just able to do beyond what we ask, but he will do abundantly beyond what we can even conceive in our minds. But that's not enough; He is able to do exceedingly abundantly beyond what we ask or think. Now, what is it that you need? Build up your faith so that God can work with the power within you to make it come to pass. Get outrageous with your faith and ask God to do far beyond what you can think. We have not because we ask not! You have to think way outside the box to get the bigger blessing. This is not the time to be realistic with your request. You can't look at your current situation or circumstances to make this happen. You have to reach for moon and beyond to even come close to what God has in store for you. So get ready for you blessing and prepare yourself for the miracles. Just make sure to give Him the glory, honor and praise

You are blessed to be a Blessing!

> *My prayer for you today is that you will think bigger than you have ever before and ask God for that supernatural blessing that you deserve and desire to receive!*

September 27

Your scripture for today:

1 John 5:14-15

This is the confidence we have in approaching God, that if we ask anything according to his will, he hears us, whatever we ask, we know that we have what we asked of him.

Observation:

Have you ever felt like God didn't hear your prayer? Sometimes God is silent and you may be in a holding pattern. That doesn't mean that He did not hear your prayer. I took a flight to Burbank and while we were in the air approaching the airport the Pilot came on the speaker to inform us that due to the stormy weather the flight would have to land at the Los Angeles airport which is still in the area but would be a little further for my daughter to pick me up. However, I could tell that the flight was in a holding pattern because I could see that we were circling the same area. Finally the Pilot came on the speaker to make us aware that the storm had passed and we would still be able to land in Burbank. So even though we had a delay and may have had a slight detour I was still able to reach my destination. Just know that God hears your prayers and wants you to get to your destination the delay could mean that you have more to learn in the place that you are in before He gives you your next move. Be still and know that He is God and that he has heard your prayer. Be confident God is listening!

You are blessed to be a Blessing!

My prayer for you today is that you will hold on and be patient while God is working things out for the best blessing you have ever had!

Your scripture for today:

Romans 8:18

I consider that our present sufferings are not worth comparing with the glory that will be revealed in us.

Observation:

You must understand that all the trials, problems, difficult situations, and unpleasant circumstances you encounter are all preparation for promotion. They will not keep you from your Destiny! They will make you stronger, they will increase your faith, they will bring you out and you will be a totally different person. Just keep moving toward God in the midst of the trials. Keep confessing the word and communicating with your Father. The glory will be revealed in you! So remember weeping may endure for a night but JOY comes in the morning!

You are blessed to be a Blessing!

> *My prayer for you today is that you understand that you are an overcomer because God has walked out your footsteps before beginning of time and He has already given you the victory in Jesus Christ!*

September 29

Your scripture for today:

1 Thessalonians 5:18

**Be thankful in all circumstances, for this is God's
will for you who belong to Christ Jesus.**

Observation:

*You may not be able to control every circumstance that happens to you,
but you can control how you react to it. Give thanks for everything so
that all things will work together for your good. When you can control
your reactions and look for what you can be thankful for your outlook
will be different. It's Gods will for us to be thankful in all situations.
When you allow life to beat you down and you complain and have a
negative attitude because you feel that life is totally unfair to you. You
are allowing yourself to get caught up under your circumstances! Don't
get caught under the circumstances! Get up, ask God what is it I am
supposed to learn from this and God will take that adversity and turn
it into prosperity! He's working it all out for your good so be thankful
at all times!*

You are blessed to be a Blessing!

*My prayer for you today is that you will be thankful
in all situations and allow God to take care of you in
whatever circumstances you find yourself in!*

September 30

Your scripture for today:

Ruth 2:12

"May the LORD repay you for what you have done. May you be richly rewarded by the LORD, the God of Israel, under whose wings you have come to take refuge."

Observation:

You may be doing things for everyone and feeling like there is no reward. But you must remember that God sees all that you are doing whether people acknowledge it or not. You will reap all that you are sowing into the lives of those you love. Keep your faith and don't let bitterness or discouragement enter in. Your reward is coming! Ruth was diligent and faithfully helped her mother-in-law without even knowing that others were talking about how she was being a blessing. You never know who is watching you and praising you for your good works. Keep being a blessing and you will always receive tremendous rewards from your Father in Heaven!

You are blessed to be a Blessing!

My prayer for you today is that you will continue to be a blessing to those in need!

OCTOBER

October 1

Your scripture for today:

2 Chronicles 14:11

Then Asa called to the LORD his God and said, "LORD, there is no one like you to help the powerless against the mighty. Help us, LORD our God, for we rely on you, and in your name we have come against this vast army. LORD, you are our God; do not let mere mortals prevail against you."

Observation:

When we make a solid decision about anything God honors that decision and sends his angels to do what we ask when we ask him for it. It's good to cry out to God in prayer. He wants you to rely on Him to deliver you out of any situation you are in. He will fight your battle for you no matter how big it seems in the natural realm. It might look like the enemy has you cornered and there is no way out, but God has supernatural power and will be victorious and will prevail. When you pray and ask God to assist you, stick to your request, don't allow doubt to enter in your thoughts or speak it out of your mouth, and expect it to come to pass. It is done!

You are blessed to be a Blessing!

My prayer for you today is that you will cry out to God your Father for all the help you need. He wants you to rely on Him to bring your victory to pass!

October 2

Your scripture for today:

Judges 2:10

**After that whole generation had been gathered to
their ancestors, another generation grew up who knew
neither the LORD nor what he had done for Israel.**

Observation:

*We have to be mindful that if we do not share what the Lord has done
for us, we will have an entire generation that can come up not knowing
the goodness of the Lord and what He has done for His children. When
Jesus walked the earth the Apostles were able to be there and see with
their eyes the power of God. We also have been eyewitnesses to his
majesty. Every time we ask, believe, and receive his goodness, we are
experiencing his Majestic power and seeing with our own eyes the
miracles he performs every day! Make sure you share the blessings with
the young people. Let them know how God has given the victory and
help you get through so many situations in your life. You might think
they are too young but they will remember just make sure you share!*

You are blessed to be a Blessing!

*My prayer for you today is that you will share all the good news
of God to your loved ones and all who are willing to listen!*

October 3

Your scripture for today:

Deuteronomy 1:11

**May the LORD, the God of your ancestors, increase you
a thousand times and bless you as he has promised!**

Observation:

*Isn't it amazing how God will come to you and help you in the area
that you think you are weak? When you go to Him with what you
might think you need to increase in He will multiple it so you are a
thousand times better than before. Have you ever tried to do something
in your own power and got frustrated and confused? That's what
Moses thought he had to do when God called him to lead the people.
He couldn't even imagine why God chose him to lead the people out of
Egypt. But when you stay close to God, our source, you are able to do
powerful and amazing things. Sometimes you amaze yourself but you
must realize that God can increase your abilities! But the key is to be
led by the Spirit of God and you can do all things and bear much fruit!*

You are blessed to be a Blessing!

> *My prayer for you today is that you will allow God
> to lead you and increase you with super natural
> power a thousand times greater than before!*

October 4

Your scripture for today:

John 15:7

**If you remain in me and my words remain in you,
ask whatever you wish, and it will be given you.**

Observation:

When you go to shop from catalog you know that you should be able to get whatever is listed. When you go to a restaurant and order from the menu you know that you should be able to get whatever is in the menu. God has left us with an entire book of promises that he is willing to fulfill, all you have to do is ask using his words and it will be given to you! The main thing is that you get to know what is in the book. When your request line up with the promises that God has already predestined for you to receive you will have whatever you ask! In the same way, if your child comes and ask you for something using the words that you may have promised them, all you can do is say, 'ok I'll do it!' Be assured that your Father God will do it for you!

You are blessed to be a Blessing!

*My prayer for you today is that you will get to know
the word of God and know all the promises and
benefits that are there for you to receive!*

October 5

Your scripture for today:

1 Peter 4:10-11

Each one should serve others, faithfully administering God's grace in its various forms. If anyone speaks, he should do it as one speaking the very words of God. If anyone serves, he should do it with the strength God provides, so that in all things God may be praised through Jesus Christ. To him be the glory and the power forever and ever. Amen.

Observation:

God gives us each gifts that we can use to serve others. Yours may be different than mine but they are designed to administer God's grace to others. If you look at the job or career that you are doing you more than likely have to service a customer. Even if you are not in the service industry, the business you work for or maybe even own is supplying a need in one capacity or another. You might not interface with the end user but what you do is important to make everything work! Just know that you are valuable and there is a reason you are doing what you do. As you work and serve; others will glorify God because of you! So keep your spirit up and God will supply the strength you need to continue to serve others!

You are blessed to be a Blessing!

My prayer for you today is that you will continue to serve others with the strength that God gives you!

October 6

Your scripture for today:

1 Corinthians 9:24

Do you not know that in a race all the runners run, but only one gets the prize? Run in such a way as to get the prize.

Observation:

We are all winners in Christ! Live like a person who has the victory. Speak like a champion. Walk with confidence. Being a winner starts inside you. What do you think about yourself? Do you encourage yourself? Don't look for others to lift you up God has already crowned you with a crown of favor. You don't need anyone else to validate you. Remember you are running in God's race and he is a powerful force behind you that is pushing you to victory. The prize is yours, so act like the winner that you are!

You are blessed to be a Blessing!

My prayer for you today is that you will run your race with confidence and that God will provide you with the victory! You are a winner in Jesus!

October 7

Your scripture for today:

1 Thessalonians 4:11-12

Make it your ambition to lead a quiet life, to mind your own business and to work with your hands, just as we told you, so that your daily life may win the respect of outsiders and so that you will not be dependent on anybody.

Observation:

Years ago there was a popular television show where there was a very nosy neighbor. She was always watching to see what she could see happening with everyone around her. You might know someone like that, who always want to know the latest gossip and love to keep drama going. To them life is boring if there isn't any issues or confusion going on. What they don't realize is that is not life at all. Because God wants you to be at peace in your life and to be his representatives here on earth, so that without saying a word others will be able to see His goodness through the examples of your daily life! That is when He is able to bless the work of your hands. He is not going to bless your messiness. But He will take the mess and turn it into a message for you to bless others and bring you the life of abundance!

You are blessed to be a Blessing!

My prayer for you today is that you will live a peaceful life and allow God to bless your life with abundance!

October 8

Your scripture for today:

1 Thessalonians 5:18

Be thankful in all circumstances, for this is God's will for you who belong to Christ Jesus.

Observation:

Without even thinking about it my prayers are always thanking God for everything. Even in the midst of problem I thank God for the answer because I know He has already solved it and can give the wisdom to get through it. When there is a financial need I thank God for being my source and my provider. Thanking Him for the money that is coming into my life. When healing is needed I thank Him for Jesus laying every disease on the cross at Calvary because by His stripes we are healed. In everything give thanks so that all things will work together for your good because you love God; therefore, every occurrence may be a subject of gratitude and thankfulness. As you put God first and have an attitude of gratitude, prosperity and adversity will be equally helpful to you!

You are blessed to be a Blessing!

> *My prayer for you today is that you will just remember to say thank you to the Father at all times no matter what is happening find something to be thankful for and it will change the outcome and your outlook! Thank you Lord!*

October 9

Your scripture for today:

Ecclesiastes 11:4-5

Whoever watches the wind will not plant; whoever looks at the clouds will not reap. As you do not know the path of the wind, or how the body is formed in a mother's womb, so you cannot understand the work of God, the Maker of all things.

Observation:

If you tried to figure out everything that's going to happen before you make a move you would never do anything at all. If you live your life always asking the "what if" question you will stay in the place that you are with no growth. You might ask; what if I try this and it doesn't work out? I have found that the "what if" question is usually a negative thought based out of fear! Change that thought into a positive! God didn't put us here to stay stuck in a rut and never change. We become too analytical for our own good. It is time to stop waiting on things to be totally right in our lives before we act on the dreams and desires God has placed in our hearts. If we look at what's going on around us we will never make a step to do anything different. Take a step of faith and trust that God's got your back. Your instructions will come as you take a step toward your goal. Trust in God and His ability to lead you to your destiny!

You are blessed to be a Blessing!

> *My prayer for you today is that you will lean not on your own understanding but acknowledge your God and allow Him to direct your path!*

October 10

Your scripture for today:

Acts 2:28

**You have made known to me the paths of life;
you will fill me with joy in your presence!**

Observation:

The only way that God can make anything known to you is by you spending time in His presence. Do you set aside time to hear from your Creator? Life is so busy and time seems to go so fast. It seems like we just celebrated the New Year and it's already just 3 months away. Where does the time go? If you don't purposely set aside time to spend with God it will not happen. God wants you to seek him to discover what path you should take. Instead of going to other people, go to your creator and ask for direction. You should know that he has already gone before you making your crooked places straight and he is just waiting for you to stop and ask for help! His way is the way to joy!

You are blessed to be a Blessing!

My prayer for you today is that you will make time for God so that He can give you the instructions you need to prosper in this life!

October 11

Your scripture for today:

Psalms 84:11

For the LORD God is a sun and shield: the LORD will give grace and glory: no good thing will He withhold from them that walk uprightly.

Observation:

As a child of the Most High God, you are assured of good things. While there will be times of trouble, God is more than enough. He is able to be whatever you need Him to be, when you need Him to be it. He will brighten your day and also protect you from hurt, harm and danger. God did not form you to live shackled. He did not purpose you to walk in depression. The enemy desires to keep you in darkness. His purpose is to keep your eyes closed to the light shining ahead. But God is shining His light for you and it is brighter than ever. He is faithful to bring you through and make sure you are protected. Today be determined to have an attitude of excitement! It doesn't matter how bad you think it is, just believe your God is greater than your storm!

You are blessed to be a Blessing!

My prayer for you today is that you will believe that God has you covered. His light is shining on your life and He is determined to make you great! Thank God for all the wonderful blessings He has in store for you!

October 12

Your scripture for today:

Proverbs 16:9

**In their hearts humans plan their course, but
the LORD establishes their steps.**

Observation:

*Have you ever experienced drastic changes in your life because the
Lord has something totally different for you to do? Just when you
became comfortable with life, the Lord says it's time to move. It's time
for a change. Do you believe that God knows what He is doing? My
family and I have moved 7 times for new career opportunities. Not just
across town but to a whole new city, state or country! Relocating is not
just moving your furniture, it's moving your entire life. From schools,
to your church, to your friends, your favorite grocery store, hair stylist,
doctor, dentist, everything must change in the new location. But what
I have found is that when God requires you to change your direction,
there is a divine purpose behind it. When He steps in and changes
your walk, do not become bitter but rejoice in the Lord. Many people
will be impacted because God led you their way. So thank God for
all the changes and moves that He orchestrates in your life, because
operating by your own rules and ways will only delay the progress and
the promise that God has for you!*

You are blessed to be a Blessing!

*My prayer for you today is that you will be open to any and every
change that is prompted by the Lord. You will be abundantly blessed
when you allow Him to guide you to the new opportunities!*

October 13

Your scripture for today:

Numbers 23:19

**God is not like people. He tells no lies. He is not like humans.
He doesn't change his mind. When he says something,
he does it. When he makes a promise, he keeps it.**

Observation:

*God promised to never leave you or forsake you! He promised to give
you the desires of your heart! He promised to give you abundant life! He
promised to give you strength when you are weak! He promised to be a
shelter, a strong tower, a place to run in time of need! He promised to
guide your footsteps and make your crooked places straight if you lean
not to your own understanding and acknowledge him! He promised to
be your healer and He promised that no good thing would He withhold
from you! Praise God for all his wonderful promises and believe that
He will make them happen in your life. His word is His bond! He said
it, so it is so! Don't think about the people you know who have made
promises to you and never kept them! That is not your God. He is not
a man and cannot be compared to any man! Don't get it twisted! If
God said it than we can believe that it will come to past. Our job is to
trust and believe that all His promises are for you!*

You are blessed to be a Blessing!

*My prayer for you today is that you believe
that the promises of God are for you!*

Your scripture for today:

Ecclesiastes 3:1

**To everything there is a season, and a time
to every purpose under the heaven.**

Observation:

There is an exact time for every blessing in our lives. Along with the exact time, there is an exact purpose associated with the blessing. The Lord knows when, where and how to bless you. He knows what you can handle, when you can handle it. Just because the answer has not come (yet) does not mean the Lord has forgotten about you. Be patient and continue to do the things that God has instructed you to do. Be thankful in whatever season you find yourself in and God will make sure that you will come out victorious!

You are blessed to be a Blessing!

> *My prayer for you today is: Lord keep us through the
> seasons of life and help us to be patient, trusting that
> you will bring us through with the victory!*

October 15

Your scripture for today:

1 Corinthians 13:4-8

Love is patient, love is kind. I does not envy, it does not boast, it is not proud. It is not rude, it is not self-seeking, it is not easily angered, it keeps no record of wrongs. Love does not delight in evil but rejoices with the truth. It always protects, always trusts, always hopes, and always perseveres. Love never fails.

Observation:

Have you ever been in love with someone? There are different phases of the love cycle that you might experience, the bottom line is that you know that you love them. Maybe you have experienced the love for your child. There are things that you might deal with because of your unconditional love for them. When you think about the fact that God is Love and you read this scripture you can better understand who our Father is. He is patient and kind, he does not envy or boast but we can sing His praises. Isn't it wonderful that God doesn't keep any records of the things we do wrong? God rejoices in the truth and protects us and never fails! If you are questioning which way to go, follow the way of love! Because it never fails! God sent his son for us because he loves us that much. There is no greater love than the love of our Father because God is LOVE!

You are blessed to be a Blessing!

My prayer for you today is that you will understand the love of God and recognize that He is madly in love with us!

October 16

Your scripture for today:

Hebrews 11:6

But without faith it is impossible to please him: for he that comes to God must believe that he is, and that he is a rewarder of them that diligently seek him.

Observation:

There is a miracle in your faith! Many people never understand how important faith is in the life of a Believer. Faith allows you to believe even when you don't see any evidence with your natural eyes! When you find yourself in need of a miracle, you have to develop a persevering attitude having faith to know that with God all things are possible. Like the dollar bill is the currency on the earth, faith is the currency in heaven. That is why you can see people with big faith become so successful on earth. Their faith allows God to increase them and bring them into a life of abundance. Diligently seek God, have faith that He will reward you, and your life will flow with blessings and miracles that you haven't even seen yet! Your best is still yet to come!

You are blessed to be a Blessing!

My prayer for you today is that your faith will be rewarded by God with overflow blessings and miracles every day!

October 17

Your scripture for today:

2 Corinthians 5:20

**We are therefore Christ's ambassadors, as though
God were making his appeal through us. We implore
you on Christ's behalf; Be reconciled to God.**

Observation:

*Reconcile means to get together again as friends. God wants us to tell
everyone of the goodness of God so that they can be God's friends just
like we are. So what is the job of an Ambassador? An Ambassador is
usually a high ranking official that is sent to represent and oversee a
particular mission. The Ambassador has been picked for the mission
because they believe in the purpose and has a passion to see it succeed.
As Christ's ambassadors we are called to reconcile others back to
God. You are His representatives here on earth with a mission that is
lead and directed by Him. If you are in Christ you are automatically
appointed to be His Ambassador so hold your head up and share the
good news to others about the God that we serve!*

You are blessed to be a Blessing!

*My prayer for you today is that you will take your appointed position
as the Ambassador for Christ and reconcile others back to God!*

October 18

Your scripture for today:

Revelation 3:20

**Behold, I stand at the door, and knock: if any man
hear My voice, and open the door, I will come in to
him, and will sup with him, and he with Me.**

Observation:

*Yes we know God could open the door Himself. Yes we know God
could knock the door down. But that's not like the Lord. We have
to be responsible enough to open the door and invite Him in! Don't
wait until things are going wrong in your life before you ask God to
intervene. Don't wait until hours before the due date before you ask
God to provide for you. Don't wait until you've fallen into sin or the
traps of the enemy before you ask God to rescue you. God will only
intervene if you ask Him to.*

You are blessed to be a Blessing!

*My prayer for you today is that you will open the door to God
when he calls you and allow Him to lead and guide your life!*

October 19

Your scripture for today:

Isaiah 59:1

**Surely the arm of the LORD is not too short to save,
nor his ear too dull to hear.**

Observation:

My grandson lost his toy car the other day and was searching all over for it. He finally saw that it was pretty far under the couch and he was trying desperately to retrieve it but his arm was just too short. So he asked for assistance to reach under the coach to get his car. I reached under and got it and he was so thankful that I saved his car! That is how God is to us. You might be trying to handle your situation not realizing that you are limited in your abilities. But, through depression, loneliness, and low self-esteem, the Lord is able to deliver you. When you are crying and reaching out for help, the Lord is able to hear and save you. God hears your whisper! Many people will never experience what you have experienced in life. Some would never recover from what you endured. God hears you when your body is tired and your voice is weak. He is able to hear what no one else hears. He is able to be strong when you are weak. God is a good God, and you are #1 in His book!

You are blessed to be a Blessing!

My prayer for you today is that you will remember that God is able to save you from anything you might be experiencing. He will comfort and protect you. Thank you God for your loving kindness!

October 20

Your scripture for today:

Psalms 91:1

**He that dwells in the secret place of the most High
shall abide under the shadow of the Almighty.**

Observation:

*Any person you claim to love is a person you spend personal time
with. It is impossible for anyone to claim they love God and never
spend any personal, intimate time with Him. How would you feel if
your companion claimed to love you, but never had any time for you?
Decide to spend quality time with the Lord. You need to have time
uninterrupted by people or materialistic distractions. You need time
when you rest in the presence of God. Time when the only thing you
care about is hearing God's voice. Time in your secret place when you
realize what you are in need of will only come from the Lord Himself.*

You are blessed to be a Blessing!

*My prayer for you today is that you will make time
to spend with Almighty God every day!*

October 21

Your scripture for today:

Luke 1:37

For with God nothing shall be impossible.

Observation:

Remember the movie Mission Impossible? There was always a message sent to the agent describing the mission which always seemed to be an impossible task. But the agent would always go to the home office and get equipped with the most creative inventions to help him accomplish that mission and he always did! He would have extreme confidence in his ability to get it done because he had experienced impossible missions before and he was fully equipped to handle it. You might be looking at your situation thinking that it is impossible but when you sit around worrying about your bills, your job, your marriage, your children, your finances, you are actually sitting around doubting the Lord. In your eyes, a positive outcome is impossible because you cannot see how things can or will get better. Worry is the opposite of faith! Faith allows you to believe even though you have not seen the manifestation yet. *God has equipped you to do impossible things because you have Him in you! You can get through and do all things including the ones that appear to be impossible. For with God nothing is impossible!*

You are blessed to be a Blessing!

> *My prayer for you today is that you will understand that*
> *God is all powerful and can handle anything you face!*

October 22

Your scripture for today:

Proverbs 8:17

**I love them that love me; and those that
seek me early shall find me.**

Observation:

*Have you ever heard someone say or found yourself saying, "I guess all
I can do is pray"? You have exhausted everything possible and now as
a final straw it's time to seek God. What you must realize is the answer
you need is found in the Lord. The guidance you seek comes through
the Lord. The void in your life can be filled by the Lord. Seek Him first
and all these things will be added to your life.*

You are blessed to be a Blessing!

*My prayer for you today is: Lord help us all to seek your face in
every situation, knowing that you are our God and you care about
everything that concerns us! We will seek you first in all that we do!*

October 23

Your scripture for today:

Luke 6:38

Give and you will receive. Your gift will return to you in full—pressed down, shaken together to make room for more, running over, and poured into your lap. The amount you give will determine the amount you get back.

Observation:

In order for you to continue receiving, you must learn how to give. So often we think we can store away all the many things God has blessed us with. But as you realize how blessed you are, you also have to understand that you are blessed to share with other people. It's not always money! It can be a gift or talent that God has given you that you are not sharing. Remember a closed hand is not ready to receive! Open your hands, give, and receive God's overflow of blessings!

You are blessed to be a Blessing!

My prayer for you today is that you live to
give! You can't beat God giving!

October 24

Your scripture for today:

Romans 1:17

The good news shows how God makes people right with himself. From beginning to end, becoming right with God depends on a person's faith. It is written, "Those who are right with God will live by faith."

Observation:

Whatever God's purpose is for your life it is going to require you to have faith to accomplish it. God has given each of us the measure of faith that we need to pursue the purpose that we are here for. As we walk through this life there will be many steps and with every step faith is required. Remember we don't have to see the whole staircase just take the first step and God will reveal the next, and the next, and the next!

You are blessed to be a Blessing!

My prayer for you today is that you understand that you must believe that God has given you a divine purpose and with faith you will be able to fulfill your destiny!

October 25

Your scripture for today:

Ecclesiastes 7:14

When times are good, be happy; but when times are bad, consider: God has made the one as well as the other. Therefore, a man cannot discover anything about his future.

Observation:

Consider the fact that God knows what is and what will be! We have been given the present as a gift to appreciate and make the most of. If we are constantly trying to figure out what is to come, we miss out on our present! I was at a football game and the quarterback threw the ball right to the receiver, but he dropped the ball. On the instant replay it was clear to see that before he actually had the ball secured he was taking off to run. He needed to receive the present then take off for the future. There is power in now! Rejoice and be glad in it!

You are blessed to be a Blessing!

> *My prayer for you today is that you will be happy*
> *in the present and not worry about tomorrow*
> *because tomorrow is already taken care of!*

October 26

Your scripture for today:

Romans 10:17

So then faith comes by hearing, and hearing by the word of God.

Observation:

We hear so many things through so many different forms of technology. The radio, television, telephone, IPod, etc. But are you taking the time to hear the word of God? The great thing is that you can hear the word through most forms of technology but it is our choice to tune into that station, stream it in, or upload it. Your faith will grow by hearing the word of God. It will build your faith as you understand more and more who God is to you, what He says about you, and how much he loves you! So take time to hear the word of faith today!

You are blessed to be a Blessing!

*My prayer for you today is that you will listen to
the word of God and allow it to sink into your spirit
as much as possible to build up your faith!*

October 27

Your scripture for today:

Nahum 1:7

**The Lord is good, a refuge in times of trouble.
He cares for those who trust in him.**

Observation:

Trust God enough to give your cares, concerns, problems, issues, and test to him. Have you ever been in a situation where you knew the answer to something and the person needing the answer never asked you? If you are a parent you know what it's like to see your child asking everyone else for advice and not you. The interesting thing is that many times the person that your child is asking may tell them the same thing you have told them before but it sounds better coming from another voice. That's how we are sometime with God. He will give us a nudge in our spirit and we second guess it until He has to send the same message through another source before you get it. Well God is our loving father and wants to be our refuge. He cares and wants to help! Trust that He has the answers you need at all times!

You are blessed to be a Blessing!

*My prayer for you today is that you will allow God
to give you what you need at all times!*

Your scripture for today is:

Romans 12: 10

Love one another with brotherly affection [as members of one family], giving precedence and showing honor to one another.

Observation:

We are members of one family, not strangers to each other. As Christians we are not isolated units; we are brothers and sisters, because we have one father, God. So we should develop the close and affectionate relationship that should exist among brothers and sisters who are blood relatives. The blood that binds us to one another as believers is even more precious! It's the blood that give us strength from day to day and it will never lose its power to bind us together in Love!

You are blessed to be a Blessing!

My prayer for you today is that you will love your brothers and sisters in Christ because we are all in the family of God!

October 29

Your scripture for today:

Deuteronomy 1:28

**Where can we go? Our brothers have made our hearts
melt in fear. They say, 'The people are stronger and
taller than we are; the cities are large, with walls up
to the sky. We even saw the Anakites there.'"**

Observation:

*After reading this passage is there any wander why they wandered in
the wilderness for 40 years? You can feel the fear they had. Everything
is better, bigger, and stronger than them. They even put down God
and said He brought them out of bondage to kill them in the desert!
Murmuring and complaining will only prolong your situation! When
you complain you remain! But when you change the way you see things
and look for the treasure in the trial, God is able to bring you out into
the promise land. When you praise you raise!*

You are blessed to be a Blessing!

*My prayer is that you will see things in a positive light. Don't
get caught murmuring and complaining about the things
you see! Praise and thank God for all that is to come!*

October 30

Your scripture for today:

Isaiah 45:3

I will give you the treasures of darkness, riches stored in secret places, so that you may know that I am the Lord the God of Israel, who summons you by name.

Observation:

God sends opportunities our way and even though we have been praying for a breakthrough we overlook it because it isn't what we think it's supposed to be. The riches stored in secret places may be right under your nose or have already been offered to you, but God will not force it on you. Be willing to try new things and put your faith out there, take the first step and God will show you the next one, and the next one, and the next one!

You are blessed to be a Blessing!

> *My prayer for you today is that you will open your eyes to new possibilities as God shows you the opportunities that you might have never thought of for yourself!*

October 31

Your scripture for today:

Romans 12:2

And be not conformed to this world: but be ye transformed by the renewing of your mind, that ye may prove what is that good, and acceptable, and perfect, will of God.

Observation:

When you see a caterpillar it is in the stage in its life before the transformation takes place. It will go through various stages before it is fully transformed into a beautiful butterfly! As new Christians we are transformed everyday by renewing our minds. The more we study the word and get it in our spirit we are transforming into all that God wants us to be. We begin to understand how God is good to us and he loves us unconditionally. He is our rock, our provider, our Lord, our Savior, Our redeemer and our deliverer. He makes a way out of no way. He heals our bodies, and gives us eternal life. We need to be thankful for all that He has done and is doing in us. Stay hungry for God and He will continue to provide a buffet of blessings for you! Just be determined to renew your mind and you will experience God's perfect will in your life!

You are blessed to be a Blessing!

My prayer for you today is that you will renew your mind and transform into the beautiful butterfly and receive all the blessings that God has for you!

NOVEMBER

November 1

Your scripture for today:

Philippians 4:17

**Not that I am looking for a gift. But I am looking
for what may be credited to your account.**

Observation:

*Every day you might hear advertisements for a free credit report or
offering you a way to fix your credit! In this society having good credit
means you can buy a home, a car, and some employer's even look at
your credit report to determine if you are accountable and reliable
enough to handle your own affairs. God credits your account when you
do good to others, when you give, when you share your love, when you
say a kind word, when you share his word, when you smile, when you
show that you care, and when you are living the life that he purposed
you to live. What is being credited to your account? Take some time
today and add more credits to your heavenly account by doing good
things on earth. Make sure that when God looks at your heavenly
credit report it is all good!*

You are blessed to be a Blessing!

*My prayer for you today is that your credit report is excellent! Do
random acts of kindness and add more credits to your account!*

November 2

Your scripture for today:

Matthew 6:25-27

**Therefore I tell you, do not worry about your life, what you
will eat or drink; or about your body, what you will wear.
Is not life more important than food, and the body more
important than clothes? Look at the birds of the air, they do
not sow or reap or store away in barns, and yet your heavenly
Father feeds them. Are you not much more valuable than they?
Who of you by worrying can add a single hour to his life?**

Observation:

*God has given us the ability to imagine and think which both are great to
have. When they are used the right way we are able to create wonderful
things. However, when used to worry it is negative meditation creating
fear of the unknown instead of faith in the possibilities. What you
think about you bring about. When you are worried about something
it will either stop you in your tracks or you will do like Abraham and
Sarah who tried to help God out and do things their way. Abraham was
clearly given the vision from God and was shown how his descendants
would be as vast as the stars in the sky. He just needed to believe that
God would bring it to past. Decide to use your imagination to think
positive thoughts and trust that God will not leave you or forsake you!
You can't listen to the negative people around you who will try to talk
you into worrying. Keep your faith and meditate on the possibilities!*

You are blessed to be a Blessing!

*My prayer for you today is that you will put your worries
aside and meditate on all the positive things that God
has done for you and will do for you in the future!*

November 3

Your scripture for today:

Psalm 37:25-26

I was young and now I am old, yet I have never seen the righteous forsaken or their children begging bread. They are always generous and lend freely; their children will be blessed.

Observation:

Haven't you seen families that are just blessed? The parents are blessed and the children are also. From generation to generation great things happen in their lives. On the other side of it you can see families where it seems that drama and bad things continue to happen from generation to generation. But I believe God can and will bring up one that will break that pattern. The power of one person that is righteous and walking with God can make a difference and change the lives of an entire generation! What a legacy to pass on! All God wants us to do is to live an upstanding life, walk with Him, talk with Him, and live to give! You will always have all that you need and more because you are a vessel that God can use to bless others. You can be the one to lead your loved ones to the Lord. You can be the one to change a generational curse to generational blessings.

You are blessed to be a Blessing!

My prayer for you today is that you will live to give and be a powerful blessing in the lives of everyone around you!

November 4

Your scripture for today:

Genesis 18:13-14

Then the LORD said to Abraham, "Why did Sarah laugh and say, 'Will I really have a child, now that I am old?' Is anything too hard for the LORD? I will return to you at the appointed time next year, and Sarah will have a son."

Observation:

Sarah was no different than most people. Have you ever shared a vision or dream that God gave you and had someone laugh because they can't believe it can happen? Or maybe it was you who laughed at that dream because when you look at the situation and circumstances it appears to be no way it can come to past! Is anything too hard for the Lord? Remind yourself that if God brought you the vision He will also give you the provision to make it happen. The Lord didn't care about how old Sarah or Abraham was. But what He did care about was their faith, trust and belief that what He said is what He would do! He said at the appointed time it would happen because even though they were old they still had some growing to do in their faith in order to see the manifestation of that promise! Don't laugh at the promises of God because of your unbelief it will only delay the blessings. So be a believer and not a doubter and you will see your dream come to past!

You are blessed to be a Blessing!

My prayer for you today is that you will believe that every dream and vision that God brings to you is sure because nothing is too hard for God!

November 5

Your scripture for today:

Ephesians 6:12

For our struggle is not against flesh and blood, but against the rulers, against the authorities, against the powers of this dark world and against the spiritual forces of evil in the heavenly realms.

Observation:

Because we are children of the light there will be forces of darkness that will try to come against us. It may seem like it's the people that we see in the physical realm who are causing difficulties in our lives. Just remember that it's not flesh and blood that is the problem but it's easy to look at it that way because that's what we see in the natural realm. But when it seems like everything is coming against you begin to pray to God to intervene in it! He will dispatch angels to fight your battle for you on a Spiritual level. You always have access to God's army; they are at your beck and call. When you recognize that evil is live spelled backward you understand that life is all about how we choose to see things. Don't concentrate on evil but turn it around and allow God to help you to live this life in the light of His blessings. God wants His children to invite His presence into their lives. Be not deceived, we cannot survive without the Lord. No matter how successful you think you are, all that you have is because of Him. He will come in if you invite Him! He will step in if you make room for His presence. Once He steps in, then He will show out on your behalf.

You are blessed to be a Blessing!

My prayer for you today is don't be moved by the evil of the darkness. You are children of the light and darkness has to go! God is fighting your battle in the spirit realm so don't be afraid!

November 6

Your scripture for today:

James 2:17-18

In the same way, faith by itself, if it is not accompanied by action, is dead. But someone will say, "You have faith; I have deeds." Show me your faith without deeds, and I will show you my faith by what I do.

Observation:

Put action to your faith! There are many who talk about what they are going to do when everything is perfect in their lives! Faith is putting what God told you to do into action whether you feel the time is right or not. We don't have God's wrist watch to know what his time says. We have to step out with blind faith because God's timing is always the right time. You don't have to be able to see how it's going to work, just have faith! If we only operate by what we see nothing new would ever be created. No records would be broken, no new inventions, because everything is created twice, first in the spiritual realm and then in the natural. You have to believe it first then act on that belief, that's when you will see it happen in your life!

You are blessed to be a Blessing!

> *My prayer for you today is that you put your faith into action and watch new things happen in your life!*

Your scripture for today:

James 4:8

Draw nigh to God, and He will draw nigh to you …

Observation:

When you decide to get to know someone and get close to them you schedule time to be with them. Even with family that you grew up with, you might have moved to a different city or gone away to school. You change and have different interest and they have also. This happened to my sister and me. We are 10 years apart and even though we talked on the phone, when I moved back to my home town after several years of living in another city, we purposely scheduled time to get together and have lunch or go to the gym together to get to know the person that we had both become. This is what we have to do when we want to draw near to God. There comes a time when everything else must be placed on hold. When your agenda and plans are submitted to the move and glory of God, do you have time? Time to read your Bible and listen to the voice of God, time to spend meditating and preparing for the assignment God has birth within you. Review your daily calendar. Look at your To-Do List. Be sure your goals for the day include spending quality time with the Master.

You are blessed to be a Blessing!

> *My prayer for you today is that you schedule time to get closer to God. He wants you to know Him and love Him!*

November 8

Your scripture for today:

3 John 1:2

Beloved, I wish above all things that you would prosper and be in health, even as your soul prospers.

Observation:

Many Believers are experiencing challenges within their bodies. But that is not God's wish! Many Believers have received negative reports from their doctors. But that is not God's wish! Many Believers are experiencing lack. But that is not God's wish! The Lord has not forgotten about you. He has heard your cry. He has noticed your tears. He has felt your pain. He has watched the disbelief of others. But, beloved, you are healed, you are Whole, and you are Prosperous! Believe it because that is God's Wish for you!

You are blessed to be a Blessing!

My prayer for you today is that you will believe the report of the Lord that says you are healed, whole, and prosperous!

November 9

Your scripture for today:

Jeremiah 1:5

Before I formed you in the womb I knew you, before you were born I set you apart; I appointed you as a prophet to the nations.

Observation:

My daughter took up baking cupcakes and really got good at it. I would watch her as she thought of a recipe that she wanted to try then get all the ingredients to begin the process of making them. She wanted them look a certain way and of course taste great! But what I noticed is that she had to begin the process with the end in mind. There were times when the recipe didn't come out the way she wanted them to but she would just start another batch. Based on the business she began to receive the end product did what it was created to do and that was to taste good so people would want more. Well God knew you and created you with the end in mind. You already have the victory because God appointed you to be a winner. Recognize that there is nothing you are going through that God didn't know was going to happen. Everything we experience is a part of our journey, but you were chosen and appointed to be great! Believe it, receive it, and declare it. You are a child of the highest God and blessed beyond measure!

You are blessed to be a Blessing!

> *My prayer for you today is that you know that you were created to be great! God already appointed you to greatness so believe it and receive it.*

November 10

Your scripture for today:

Psalm 100:1-2

**Make a joyful noise to the Lord, all you lands! Serve the Lord
with gladness! Come before His presence with singing!**

Observation:

*It's a pleasure to encounter a person that is so full of joy that it spills
over on you! I love being serviced by a person who you can tell is
obviously enjoying what they are doing. When you have that joy in
your heart there are times you just want to sing out loud because you
are bursting with gladness. I am not that great a singer but I can make
a joyful noise! It's great to enjoy every minute you have. But many of
us are headed toward a goal that we have diligently been working on
but are not enjoying the trip. It would be such a tragedy to arrive at
the end of your journey and realize you didn't enjoy life to its fullest!
You must be determined to enjoy this life every minute at a time. Don't
forget the simple things of life because they all add up to that great BIG
thing that you are dreaming of. Give praise to God for all the things He
has done and is doing to make your journey sweet!*

Make a joyful noise to the Lord!

You are blessed to be a Blessing!

*My prayer for you today is that you will learn to
enjoy your journey and make a joyful noise to the
Lord because He is good yes He is good!*

November II

Your scripture for today is:

Hebrews 4:12

For the word of God is living and active. Sharper than any double-edged sword, it penetrates even to the dividing soul and spirit, joints and marrow; it judges the thoughts and attitudes of the heart.

Observation:

I bought a set of knives from a young lady who came to my house and did a demonstration of how powerful the knives were. She showed how they would cut through ice and chop up a Melon with hardly any effort at all. I have to admit they are very sharp knives so I had to buy them and still have them to this day! One day while using one of the knives I began to think about this scripture and how the word is powerful, sharp, and goes deep into our soul. When we hear a scripture and it lifts our spirit and gives us hope we know the word is working. When we hear the word and it convicts us and causes us to repent we know the word is penetrating into our spirit! The words we speak every day create and shape our life that's how we know the word is living and active. The word of God sharpens us, matures us, gives us wisdom, develops and matures us from the inside out.

You are blessed to be a Blessing!

My prayer for you today is that you will study the word to mold and make you into the person that God wants you to be!

Your scripture for today:

Daniel 3:15-16

"Now if you are ready, at the moment you hear the sound of the horn, flute, lyre, trigon, psaltery and bagpipe and all kinds of music, to fall down and worship the image that I have made, very well. But if you do not worship, you will immediately be cast into the midst of a furnace of blazing fire; and what god is there who can deliver you out of my hands?" Shadrach, Meshach and Abed-nego replied to the king, "O Nebuchadnezzar, we do not need to give you an answer concerning this matter. "If it be so, our God whom we serve is able to deliver us from the furnace of blazing fire; and He will deliver us out of your hand, O king…

Observation:

It takes a great deal of courage to stand for what you believe no matter what you are being threatened with. The 3 young men in this story stood up to the king even being faced with being thrown in a furnace of blazing fire. They believed without a shadow of a doubt that God would deliver them and He did! God delivered them and because of their faith many were saved. Thank God for all the miracles and deeds done every day in our lives! Yes we can look back and see all the wonderful things God has done but don't forget that he is doing them right now! You serve a God that is all powerful and will deliver you out of the hands of the enemy. You don't have to bow down to any other gods! Our God is an Awesome God!

You are blessed to be a Blessing!

My prayer for you today is that you will be confident in the God you serve! He is always with you and will deliver you from the hands of the enemy!

November 13

Your scripture for today:

1 Chronicles 29:18

O Lord, the God of Abraham, Isaac, and Israel, our fathers, keep forever such purposes and thoughts in the hearts of your people, and direct their hearts toward you.

Observation:

The people in this scripture were so excited to help build the temple and give freely and joyously of the money and time to see it built. When you are a part of a team and work toward a common goal the positive energy that is shared causes everyone to win! The word TEAM stands for:

Together – Everyone – Achieves - More

I have been a member of a church that was in the midst of a building fund and one thing I noticed was as I helped and donated to build the house of God, God was in turn blessing me with all that I needed. I was receiving unexpected blessing and I knew it was because my thoughts were on the building of the Church. When you sow seed in good ground you will always reap a great harvest of blessings!

You are blessed to be a Blessing!

My prayer for you today is that you work together with others for a common cause and watch God bless the work of your hands!

November 14

Your scripture for today:

Joshua 1:8

This Book of the Law shall not depart from your mouth, but you shall meditate on it day and night, so that you may be careful to do according to all that is written in it. For then you will make your way prosperous, and then you will have good success.

Observation:

Meditating on the word is a great way to understand how God wants you to live in this life. The word is like an instruction manual that will help you build a life of success. Have you ever bought something that needed to be assembled? It always comes with an instruction manual to help you put the item together. You have to read the manual, meditate on the instructions and keep looking at the finished product pictured on the box to make sure you are getting it right. As we focus on God and meditate on His words you will receive step by step instructions on how to live the good life!

You are blessed to be a Blessing!

> *My prayer for you today is that you will meditate on the word of God day and night and be careful to do what is in it! You will be successful beyond measure!*

November 15

Your scripture for today:

Ephesians 1:15-18

Ever since I first heard of your strong faith in the Lord Jesus and your love for God's peoples everywhere, I have not stopped thanking God for you. I pray for you constantly, asking God, the glorious Father of our Lord Jesus Christ, to give you spiritual wisdom and insight so that you might grow in your knowledge of God. I pray that your hearts will be flooded with light so that you can understand the confident hope he has given to those he called his holy people who are his rich and glorious inheritance.

Observation:

What a wonderful prayer to pray for your loved ones! It will help build them up in the spirit realm every time you pray for them. Every place it says 'you or your' put the name of the person you are praying for and watch the blessings begin to flow in their lives! This is an awesome prayer to pray for you as well! Wouldn't it be awesome for others to hear about how strong your faith is? Just to think that people are talking about the love you show to others everywhere you go and the faith you have in God is a blessing. When you do for others you automatically get blessed. Others are praying for you because you have a heart for others. Don't take anything for granted but be confident in your ability and know that God is with you always!

You are blessed to be a Blessing!

My prayer for you today is that you will know the hope of your calling and the riches that you are inheriting in the kingdom of God!

November 16

Your scripture for today is:

Exodus 4:11

The LORD said to him, "Who gave human beings their mouths? Who makes them deaf or mute? Who gives them sight or makes them blind? Is it not I, the LORD? Now go; I will help you speak and will teach you what to say."

Observation:

When God presented Moses with the opportunity to rescue His people, Moses had so many excuses as to why he was not able to do it. His last excuse was that he could not speak well. God then had to let him know that He was in control of this just go! How many times do we question our own abilities and doubt that we can do great things? Can you imagine going to your Creator and telling Him what you can't do when He is the one who made you and knows exactly what He put in you and therefore knows exactly what you are capable of doing? When God gives you direction and an assignment to do, don't second guess it or doubt your abilities. He knows what He has called you to do and will help you be successful! Now go!

You are blessed to be a Blessing!

My prayer for you today is that you will be confident in your abilities to complete any assignment initiated and ordained by God.

November 17

Your scripture for today is:

Ephesians 6:13-17

Therefore put on the full armor of God, so that when the day of evil comes, you may be able to stand your ground, and after you have done everything, to stand. Stand firm then, with the belt of truth buckled around your waist, with the breastplate of righteousness in place, and with your feet fitted with the readiness that comes from the gospel of peace. In addition to all this, take up the shield of faith, with which you can extinguish all the flaming arrows of the evil one. Take the helmet of salvation and the sword of the Spirit, which is the word of God.

Observation:

If you're like me you are probably wondering how you can put all of this armor on and not be loaded down. Well this armor is in the spirit realm where you study the word to know the truth about our God. When you are determined to live your life the way that God has stipulated and walk in peace to shield against drama and strife you are putting on the armor of God. When you make the decision to be saved and study the word to show yourself approved you are putting on the armor of God. The armor might not be seen in the physical realm but others will know that you have put it on when things come against you it will bounce off you like a bullet on a bullet proof vest. It may knock you down for a moment but you will get back up again because it didn't penetrate! You will stand firm because you put your armor on!

You are blessed to be a Blessing!

My prayer for you today is that you will put on the whole armor of God and be ready to stand against anything that comes your way!

Your scripture for today:

2 Thessalonians 2:16-17

**May our Lord Jesus Christ himself and God our
Father, who loved us and by his grace gave us eternal
encouragement and good hope, encourage your hearts
and strengthen you in every good deed and word.**

Observation:

*God's love and encouragement for us never dies, it lives on, and on,
and on! Even when it seems that others don't appreciate you for the
good you are doing! God will strengthen your heart to do good anyway!
In Texas there are toll roads where you have to pay every so many miles
to continue driving on them. The toll road usually is a faster route and
a few less cars because many people don't want to pay the tolls so they
take the regular highway. So upon occasion I will not only pay my toll
but I will pay for the person behind me. It's always fun to look in the
rear view mirror and see the person's reaction. God sees the good you
do, so do good things anyway! When your positive words seem to fall
on deaf ears, speak positive words anyway! Continue to be the light
and God will bless you anyway!*

You are blessed to be a Blessing!

> *My prayer for you today is that you will do good things
> and encourage others whether they acknowledge
> it or not. God will bless you anyway!*

November 19

Your scripture for today:

Philippians 2:9-11

**Therefore God exalted him to the highest place
and gave him the name that is above every name,
that at the name of Jesus every knee should bow,
in heaven and on earth and under the earth,
and every tongue acknowledge that Jesus Christ is Lord,
to the glory of God the Father..**

Observation:

What's in a name? New parents are always faced with the issue of thinking of a name for their unborn child. Some people are very creative with the name and I have seen some very interesting ways they decided to spell the name to make it unique. This can be a joyous time for the family while they anticipate this new person that God has allowed them to birth into this world. Many first time fathers like to name their son after them to keep the name going and create a legacy. Well God gave His son the name of Jesus and he knew that at the mention of his name every knee would bow and tongue confess that he is Lord. You can call on the name of Jesus for salvation, deliverance, healing, and peace! What's in a name, everything is in the name of Jesus!

You are blessed to be a Blessing!

My prayer for you today is that you are confident in calling on the name of Jesus! There is power in that name!

November 20

Your scripture for today:

Genesis 2:2

By the seventh day God had finished the work he had been doing; so on the seventh day he rested from all his work. Then God blessed the seventh day and made it holy, because on it he rested from all the work of creating that he had done.

Observation:

God created us in His image to do the things that he does and follow his lead. Do you find yourself so busy with your life that you don't take a day to rest? He even made the seventh day a holy day to make it easier to set aside time to rest. I have been guilty of being a workaholic trying to make it happen. Until one day as I was driving in my car I heard the Spirit say just as clear as the day, "Why are you so busy? What are you trying to do? Are you allowing yourself to be replenished? Are you doing all this for your own glory or for my glory?" I actually had to pull the car over for a few minutes to think about what I had just heard. I thank God for stopping me in my tracks and making me see that there is a time to rest and be still. Take that time to let God minister to you. You will get much more done because your mind is clear and fresh so that He can give you the creative ideas you need. Take the time to rest and be refreshed!

You are blessed to be a Blessing!

> *My prayer for you today is that you will set aside a day of rest from your busy hectic schedule. Allow God to minister to you and give you all that you need to be refreshed!*

November 21

Your scripture for today:

Psalm 27:13-14

**I would have lost heart, unless I had believed that I
would see the goodness of the Lord in the land of the
living. Wait on the Lord; be of good courage, and He
will strengthen your heart, wait, I say, on the Lord!**

Observation:

*We have to stay encouraged and not lose heart. The dreams and
desires God has placed in us will come to past! Believe that God placed
that dream in your heart therefore he will help you make it happen.
We usually have a problem with the wait on the Lord part. Just like
Abraham and Sarah, we decide to help God out while we wait, just in
case He needs our help to figure out how and when the dream needs
to be completed. Remember God knows when we are ready to receive
that blessing! His timing is always best. Trust and believe and you will
have the goodness of the Lord in the land of the living!*

You are blessed to be a Blessing!

*My prayer for you today is that you will be strengthened
and encouraged to know that God is working for you
behind the scenes to make your dreams come to past!*

Your scripture for today is:

Matthew 14:22-23

Immediately Jesus made the disciples get into the boat and go on ahead of him to the other side, while he dismissed the crowd. After he had dismissed them, he went up on a mountainside by himself to pray. Later that night, he was there alone...

Observation:

Have you ever felt the need to go away and be alone with God? These are times of refreshing for you and time to listen to God. There are some people who hate to be alone. They constantly require some sort of company around them at all times. They don't like the silence and will always have noise going on around them, like the radio or television. But there are times that you need to dismiss the crowd and turn off the noise so that you can be with the Father! It doesn't have to be long but just set aside time for you and God. This will help to prepare and strengthen you on the inside for all the miracles that God wants to perform through you. The main thing to remember is that you are never alone. God is always with you!

You are blessed to be a Blessing!

My prayer for you today is that you will schedule time to be with your heavenly Father so that you will be prepared for everything and able to do all things because of His strength in you!

Your scripture for today is:

Malachi 3:7

Ever since the time of your ancestors you have turned away from my decrees and have not kept them. Return to me, and I will return to you," says the LORD Almighty.

Observation:

When you don't take the time to share with your children the goodness of the Lord and His commandments they will be lost. It's interesting how recipes can be handed down from generation to generation without a problem. You make things a certain way because that's how your Mom or Grandmother made it. But it also works in the opposite way. The sins of the father or mother can also be handed down to the children. If they have turned away from God and do things in an unrighteous way that's what they see so that's what they will do! We have to continue to pray for those who have lost their way and hope they return back to the Lord. Whenever you are lost you can always call on the Lord and he will seek you out and help you find your way back to him.

You are blessed to be a Blessing!

*My prayer for you today is that you will return
to the Lord and see that He is good!*

Your scripture for today:

I Corinthians 15:57

But thanks be to God, which gives us the victory through our Lord Jesus Christ.

Observation:

Have you ever encountered a person who was so confident in their abilities to win that they would always win? They don't brag about it they just have a confident air about them and are focused on the task at hand! They don't let doubt enter into their mind and they always have an attitude of gratitude. You are a winner no matter what you may be going through! No matter what it looks like you already have the victory because you are a child of God. When you give thanks and praise God through it all, your victory is a sure thing! Stay focused on the goal and be confident in yourself knowing that you already have the victory. So lift your head up and put your shoulders back. Walk, talk and act like the winner that you are!

Thanks be to God!

You are blessed to be a Blessing!

My prayer for you today is that you understand that the victory is yours no matter what it looks like. Thank God for the victory!

November 25

Your scripture for today is:

Lamentations 3:22-23

**Because of the LORD's great love we are not
consumed, for his compassions never fail. They are
new every morning; great is your faithfulness.**

Observation:

*Today is a new day! Thank God that with every new day He gives you
new blessings, mercy, grace, and compassion! Yesterday is old news!
The good news is that God is faithful and able to turn your mourning
into dancing! Don't rehearse the problems of your pass. Think about
and reflect on your victories and how faithful God has been to you!
Get your joy back and praise God because your best is yet to come!*

You are blessed to be a Blessing!

*My prayer for you today is that you will be thankful for
Gods faithfulness, grace, favor and mercy. Thank God that
old things are passed away and all things become new!*

Your scripture for today:

Psalm 5:11-12

But let all who take refuge in you be glad; let them ever sing for joy. Spread your protection over them that those who love your name may rejoice in you. For surely, O Lord, you bless the righteous; you surround them with your favor as with a shield.

Observation:

Did you put on your crown of favor this morning? As a child of God you have his protection love and favor! Believe that God is on your side. Where ever you are remember that He has surrounded you with his favor as you go about your day. Put your shoulders back and head up so your crown doesn't fall off your head. Think about any Queen or King and how they reflect royalty at all times. You would never see them with their head down. They know they went to bed King or Queen and they woke up the same way. It's the same for you because you are royalty in the kingdom of God. Just imagine as you go through the day that others are seeing your crown of favor because God is causing them to give you the favor that you deserve. Take some time to thank Him for His goodness and rejoice!

You are blessed to be a Blessing!

> *My prayer for you today is that you will except your*
> *rightful place in the kingdom of God and know that you*
> *can wear the crown of favor just put it on every day!*

November 27

Your scripture for today:

John 10:10

The thief comes only in order to steal and kill and destroy. I came that they may have and enjoy life, and have it in abundance (to the full, till it overflows).

Observation:

No matter what the enemy has attempted to do. I do not care what others have said about you. It doesn't even matter what trouble you currently find yourself in. In spite of it all, you are blessed. The enemy is out to destroy you and distract you because he knows God has His hand on you and your future is bright. Don't forget how truly blessed you really are. Give God a radical praise of thanksgiving today. I mean a praise that comes out of your mouth. Not just a hand clap or a thought, but a praise where words exit your mouth. He has kept you, and will continue to keep you all the days of your life! So praise Him!

You are blessed to be a Blessing!

My prayer for you today is that you will not allow the thief to steal from the abundant life that God has for you! Give praises to God for everything he has done and is doing in your life!

Your scripture for today:

Matthew 6:2-4

So when you give to the needy, do not announce it with trumpets, as the hypocrites do in the synagogues and on the streets, to be honored by others. Truly I tell you, they have received their reward in full. But when you give to the needy, do not let your left hand know what your right hand is doing, so that your giving may be in secret. Then your Father, who sees what is done in secret, will reward you.

Observation:

Have you ever been given something by someone and every time they see you with it they tell everyone that they gave it to you? It makes you want to give it back to them because they are really looking to be recognized for giving it by others. It's like they really never let it go! When God put it on your heart to give then you should give not out of necessity or recognition, but because you truly want to bless that person with it. God sees the good that you do and what you give to the needy. He also knows when you are obedient to Him and give because He told you to. It might be done in secret but God will openly reward you for being a blessing to others!

You are blessed to be a Blessing!

My prayer for you today is that you will give and truly desire to bless others with whatever God instructs you to bless them with! Your reward will come from God!

November 29

Your scripture for today is:

Matthew 5:27

When she heard about Jesus, she came up behind him in the crowd and touched his cloak, because she thought, "If I just touch his clothes, I will be healed." Immediately her bleeding stopped and she felt in her body that she was freed from her suffering.

Observation:

Is your belief strong enough to have faith that Jesus can do whatever you need Him to do? This woman had exhausted all that she knew to do to be healed. She didn't know what else to do after 12 years of suffering with this disease. Can you imagine what a blessing it was for her to hear about this healer name Jesus and the fact that he was coming to her town? I believe she fought her way through that crowd to touch whatever she could touch and she believed that she would be healed. When you have strong faith in Jesus he is able to do mighty works through you because your faith and his faith will intercept and that connection will cause powerful breakthroughs to occur. You will be free of all your suffering, pain, and despair. Just get connected with Jesus have faith and believe.

You are blessed to be a Blessing!

My prayer for you today is that you will have super faith and believe in the power of getting connected to Jesus!

November 30

Your scripture for today:

John 3:2

He came to Jesus at night and said, "Rabbi, we know that you are a teacher who has come from God. For no one could perform the signs you are doing if God were not with him."

Observation:

Jesus being the son of God was able to do some awesome and amazing things while on earth. He took time to be with the Father in prayer and meditation. He was always allowing God to lead and guide his path. That is why he would go off and be alone. He also didn't allow everyone to be in his circle. Even though he spoke to multitudes of people, he only allowed a smaller group to be in his space. When he detected any unbelief from those around him when he was about to perform a miracle, he would dismiss them and put them out. When Jesus knew he was leaving he said we would do even greater works then him. We just have to look at his example of prayer & meditation, allow God to lead, limit your circle of influence and keep the negativity far away from your life! Others will look at the things you do and know that God has to be with you!

You are blessed to be a Blessing!

My prayer for you today is that you will look to Jesus as an example of how we can be closer to God and begin to do awesome and amazing things in our life.

DECEMBER

December 1

Your scripture for today:

John 4:42

They said to the woman, "We no longer believe just because of what you said; now we have heard for ourselves, and we know that this man really is the Savior of the world."

Observation:

There comes a time in our walk with the Lord that we must believe for ourselves that he is Lord. In our household as a child we went to church all the time. There was something going on every day at the church and we would be there, either with my parents or my aunt and uncle. Back then I wondered why we had to go every day. But now I know it was giving me a strong foundation in God. Others like your parents or grandparents may have believed for you as a child but as you get older you have to believe and know beyond the shadow of a doubt that He is the Savior of the world. It's just another part of growing in spiritual maturity. It's great to hear others testimony about what the Lord has done for them but you need to experience Him for yourself!

You are blessed to be a Blessing!

My prayer for you today is that you get to know the Lord for yourself and believe that He is the Savior!

December 2

Your scripture for today:

1 Corinthians 2:9-10

However, as it is written: No eye has seen, nor ear has heard, no mind has conceived what God has prepared for those who love him but God has revealed it to us by his Spirit. The Spirit searches all things, even the deep things of God.

Observation:

If God revealed all that He wants to do for us it might just blow our minds. He knows he can only give us a little bit at a time. You must be ready to receive the goodness of God. Sometimes it comes in ways that you have not even thought of. God has prepared a life full of riches for those who love him. You can't even fathom all the blessings He has in store for you. That's why it says no eye has seen nor ear has heard neither can your mind conceive what He has prepared for you. Take the time to be alone with God and allow him to reveal it through your Spirit. He has equipped you with everything you need and will guide you to everything you desire through your Spirit.

You are blessed to be a Blessing!

My prayer for you today is that you will believe that God has so much in store for you and your best is still yet to come!

December 3

Your scripture for today:

Psalms 29:11

**The LORD gives strength to his people;
the LORD blesses his people with peace.**

Observation:

There is no need to question whether God has good things for us. He states it over and over in the word. He gives us His strength when we are weak and He wants us to be at peace. If you have ever been at a point in your life where it seems everything is happening at once and it requires your attention, you can look back and see how you had to have supernatural intervention to get it all done. When I had my second daughter and came home with her this was one of those times for me. New babies are on their own schedule and it's usually every 3 hours you need to feed them, change their diapers and just give them the comfort they need. Well we were in the midst of moving to a new city for my husband's job so while she sleep I packed and took care of my first daughter who was 4 years old. When I think about it now I know God had to give me the strength to get things done and still keep my peace. Thank God for His strength and His peace!

You are blessed to be a Blessing!

My prayer for you today is that you will recognize the strength that God gives you and His peace that no one else can give you!

December 4

Your scripture for today:

John 4:22-23

Yet a time is coming and has now come when the true worshipers will worship the Father in spirit and truth, for they are the kind of worshipers the Father seeks. God is spirit and his worshipers must worship in spirit and in truth.

Observation:

I think about how excited we are when we receive recognition for the things we do. When you spend the day cleaning the house you love to hear that it looks great. When you have made the decision to lose weight and you have changed the way you eat and worked out you love to hear when others notice your hard work because the weight is coming off. Maybe you have been working on a project at work, taking work home and working late nights at the office. You want to be recognized for the work you are doing. When we worship and praise God for all that he has done and is doing in our lives we must understanding that it is good and pleases God. Everything you have and are able to do is because of God. He just wants to be recognized just like we do. Keep praising and worshipping the Father. Be faithful and true and His blessings will over flow in your life!

You are blessed to be a Blessing!

My prayer for you today is that you will give God the recognition He deserves and praise Him at all times. He is the truth and you can worship Him is spirit and in truth!

December 5

Your scripture for today:

James 3:9

With the tongue we praise our Lord and Father, and with it we curse men, who have been made in God's likeness. Out of the same mouth come praise and cursing. My brothers this should not be. Can both fresh water and salt water flow from the same spring? My brothers, can a fig tree bear olives, or a grapevine bear figs? Neither can a salt spring produce fresh water.

Observation:

Watch what you say and understand that you have a powerful weapon; our tongue! Death and life are in the power of the tongue. Those who know me know that I never use curse words. I would spell the word out if I needed to tell someone what was said. It's not that I couldn't say the word I just didn't want to. My Mom never used curse words so I have to say that she was my role model. I have seen people who have struggled with changing that part of their vocabulary and I commend them for that. Not because it's my choice but because it's Gods choice. Choose to bless others with your words. Choose to encourage with your words. Choose to spread the good news with your words. Choose life you have the power!

You are blessed to be a Blessing!

My prayer for you today is that you will choose to use your words to bless others and not curse them.

Your scripture for today:

Psalm 145:3-4

**Great is the Lord and most worthy of praise; his greatness
no one can fathom. One generation will commend your
work to another; they will tell of your mighty acts.**

Observation:

*The Bible is full of stories about the goodness of God. The Old Testament
has so many stories about how God worked directly with His people.
The New Testament has more stories about how God worked through
Jesus to get things done on the earth and how he then passed it on to
the disciples and also to us. We now have the privilege to pass it on.
All the great and wonderful things God has done for us. We must pass
it on to the next generation. His word has lived for thousands of years
and it is up to us to continue to spread the good news by just sharing
what he has done for us individually. There is so much bad news being
spread all day, every day. So let's make sure we are telling about God's
greatness every day!*

You are blessed to be a Blessing!

> *My prayer for you today is that you will pass on
> the good news to others. Testify of the goodness of
> the Lord and all that he has done for you!*

December 7

Your scripture for today:

Psalm 107:14-15

He brought them out of darkness and the deepest gloom and broke away their chains. Let them give thanks to the Lord for his unfailing love and his wonderful deeds for men.

Observation:

There are so many times God brings us out of things that we don't even know about. But then there are those times that you know the only way you got out of that darkness was because God had to do it. He has already walked out your footsteps before you were born. He is working behind the scenes making your crooked places straight. There is nothing that you go through that He didn't already know you would go through. The key to that is that you went through it! He also knew that you would because he worked things out in your favor. Give thanks to God continually for the love that he shows for his children.

You are blessed to be a Blessing!

> *My prayer for you today is that you will thank God*
> *for all the things that he has brought you through.*
> *He is a good God who cares and loves you!*

December 8

Your scripture for today:

Psalm 142:1-3

**I cry aloud to the Lord; I lift up my voice to the Lord
for mercy. I pour out my complaint before him;
before him I tell my trouble. When my spirit grows
faint within me, it is you who knows my way.**

Observation:

*When you have trouble in your life God is the one to go to. Look to him
for your help first. Don't go ask everyone else before you go to God. Ask
that he give you wisdom to know what to do and vision to see the right
direction to go in. He knows you and what would be your best move to
make. Have you ever watched a game show on television and sitting
on your sofa you can see what the answer is? However, the game show
contestant can't see it and she is right there. Sometimes we are so close
to the situation that we can't see the forest for the trees. But God is the
one who knows all and sees it all. He will give you the insight you need
and the strength you need to stand.*

You are blessed to be a Blessing!

> *My prayer for you today is that you will run to God
> and tell Him all your trouble. He cares for you and
> will give you the strength you need to succeed!*

December 9

Your scripture for today:

Isaiah 57:15

For this is what the high and lofty one says he who lives forever, whose name is holy: "I live in a high and holy place, but also with him who is contrite and lowly in spirit, to revive the spirit of the lowly and to revive the heart of the contrite."

Observation:

We have a heavenly Father that is willing to come where we are, where ever we are! Jesus was always criticized by the religious rulers of his day for being around those who they described as unclean. Jesus was by the pool at Bethesda when he commanded the man with the infirmity to take up his bed and be healed. He went where the people needed him. If we are feeling low, he is there, if we are feeling great, he is there. When we need comfort he is there. Our God is ready and willing to roll up His sleeves and get low to bring us up!

You are blessed to be a Blessing!

My prayer for you today is that you understand that God has a heart for you no matter what you are going through! He will be with you and comfort you!

Your scripture for today:

Habbakuk 2:2-3

Then the LORD replied: "Write down the revelation and make it plain on tablets so that a herald may run with it. For the revelation waits an appointed time; it speaks of the end and will not prove false. Though it linger, wait for it; it will certainly come and will not delay.

Observation:

When God gives you a vision, write it down and meditate on it. He will give you the step by step instructions on how to get it all done. Don't worry about how it will get done. The main thing is to get started! Begin to move in the direction of the vision that was given to you and the way will become clearer with every step that you take. Keep pressing forward. Don't expect everyone to see it as clearly as you do. But with your plan written down you are the one to bring it to pass! As you complete the vision others will begin to see what God already revealed to you! Just trust, have faith, and believe!

You are blessed to be a Blessing!

My prayer for you today is that you will write the plan that God has given you and make it clear to yourself and to others that you need to make it come to pass.

December 11

Your scripture for today:

Philippians 2:3-4

**Do nothing out of selfish ambition or vain conceit,
but in humility consider others better than yourselves.
Each of you should look not only to your own
interests, but also to the interests of others.**

Observation:

*What if Jesus had selfish ambition, would he have gone to the cross
for us? When he was brought before the rulers He could have thought
about himself and said what they wanted Him to say to be saved from
the cross. But Jesus looked into the future and saw you and me and
decided to make the ultimate sacrifice. I have seen people who think
only of themselves. It's always about what's in it for them. They won't
do anything for others unless there is a benefit in it for them. God
honors those who help others. You have the ability to esteem others
and lift them up. When you do God will lift you up because you have
a heart to help others!*

You are blessed to be a Blessing!

*My prayer for you today is that you will lift up others without
selfish ambition and really desire to help see them succeed.
When you do you are in for a blessing from God!*

December 12

Your scripture for today:

Hebrews 10:35-36

So do not throw away your confidence; it will be richly rewarded. You need to persevere so that when you have done the will of God, you will receive what he has promised.

Observation:

There are times when we are working toward a goal and it looks like it's not going to happen. We can begin to get discouraged and think that it's not for us. But God sent this scripture to remind us that at that point you have to look to him and know that you will reap if you faint not. We start to look at things in the natural realm and know for sure that we can't make it happen. That is exactly right! You will never get it done without the supernatural power of God working through you and giving you grace and favor to get it done! So your confidence has to be in the God that is working in and through you. It's not by my power or might but by your Spirit Lord! Have an ABC moment; A – Adjust your Attitude, B – Believe that it will happen, and C-have Confidence in God that it will come to pass. You will receive His promise, so be happy and begin to rejoice!

You are blessed to be a Blessing!

My prayer for you today is that you will adjust your attitude, believe and make sure you have confidence in God. ABC it's easy!

December 13

Your scripture for today:

Romans 4:17

**As it is written: "I have made you a father of many
nations." He is our father in the sight of God, in
whom he believed—the God who gives life to the
dead and calls into being things that were not.**

Observation:

*If you were to write about your faith what would you write? Abraham
had every reason in the natural to doubt that what God told him would
not happen. But he believed that if God said it, it would happen. God
can revive your dream and bring it to life. You must call the things
that are not as though they were until they are! Take the time to think
of things you have done because you believed and had faith .Rehearse
them, meditate on them, and as you do your faith will increase because
you will bring to your mind what God has done in the past and will do
again! Keep believing and have faith in God!*

You are blessed to be a Blessing!

> *My prayer for you today is that you will build up your faith
> and believe that if God gave you a promise, it will be done!*

December 14

Your scripture for today:

1 Timothy 1:16

But for that very reason I was shown mercy so that in me, the worst of sinners, Christ Jesus might display his immense patience as an example for those who would believe in him and receive eternal life.

Observation:

Paul was shown mercy and was writing this scripture to thank God and testify about the grace that only God can give. Of all people Paul was one that you would think God would not want to save. But as the scripture states this is a powerful example of how God saves and delivers all! There is nothing you can do that would cause God to forsake you. You would have to leave Him but he will never leave you. He will not give up on you because He loves you unconditionally. Thank God for His mercy and grace that is new every morning. God is our refuge and our protection and keeps us safe in his arms.

You are blessed to be a Blessing!

My prayer for you today is that you understand that God's grace and mercy will cover you and He loves you and will save you so that you will receive eternal life!

December 15

Your scripture for today:

1 Timothy 2:1

**I urge, then, first of all, that petitions, prayers,
intercession and thanksgiving be made for all people
for kings and all those in authority, that we may live
peaceful and quiet lives in all godliness and holiness.**

Observation:

*Prayer is so important! When we pray and intercede for others it
helps to bring God's power on the scene. Every morning on my prayer
call with my prayer warriors we pray for others needs but always
pray for the leaders of our country and the rulers all over the world.
It is important to ask that they seek the wisdom of God and that
they don't pursue their own agenda. We pray that they will seek God
when making any decisions so that we can live peaceful and quiet
lives. Continue to do God's will and intercede for others and those in
authority. While others might be murmuring and complaining about
those in authority your prayers will bring power and God into the
situation at all times*

You are blessed to be a Blessing!

*My prayer for you today is that you will pray and intercede
for others and all those in authority in our lives.*

December 16

Your scripture for today:

1 Peter 4:11

If anyone speaks, he should do it as one speaking the very words of God. If anyone serves, he should do it with the strength God provides, so that in all things God may be praised through Jesus Christ. To him be the glory and the power for ever and ever. Amen.

Observation:

Realize that others see God through the things that you say and do. If you are constantly complaining it is not a good reflection of your trust and faith in the power of God in your life. He is able to do all the things you ask but it is according to the power that is at work within you. So if you have a complaining spirit it limits God's ability to work on your behalf. If you hear yourself speaking doubt and negativity have the presence of mind to change that conversation from a complaint into a positive statement that a winner would make. You are a winner so have an attitude of gratitude and watch God move to make things happen for you!

You are blessed to be a Blessing!

My prayer for you today is that you will speak words of faith, victory and blessings.

December 17

Your scripture for today:

Philippians 4:6

Do not be anxious about anything, but in everything, by prayer and petition, with thanksgiving, present your requests to God. And the peace of God, which transcends all understanding, will guard your heart and your minds in Christ Jesus.

Observation:

When you feel yourself getting anxious you have to realize that you are operating in your own power. God is sitting back waiting for you to ask Him to help. He is a patient God and will wait for your petition or request. We have not because we ask not. We have an all-powerful God at our beck and call and we try to do everything on our own. I love to call on God and see how He makes things fall into place with ease and grace. Desire to have the peace of God that is that calm, sweet, relaxed state of being that you get to have when you have totally surrendered to Him. It's that time when you exhale, and allow the Spirit to lead you. It's like floating on a raft, or laying back in a hammock on a beautiful day. We all need that peace in our lives. Just let go, and let God!

You are blessed to be a Blessing!

My prayer for you today is that you will stop the madness and call on the power of God so that you will have the peace that passes all understanding!

December 18

Your scripture for today:

Proverbs 2:7-8

**He holds success in store for the upright,
he is a shield to those whose walk is blameless,
for he guards the course of the just
and protects the way of his faithful ones.**

Observation:

God wants His people to be successful in every area of life. He shields you from being consumed by the circumstances of life and leads you to prosperity. Be faithful to God and He will be faithful to you. Be determined to move ahead. Ask God for wisdom and understanding so that you can live an upright life. It's never too late to change direction. If you have been doing things the wrong way pivot, turn around and begin to go the right way. God will guard you and protect you so that no harm will come to you. You can't lose with God because he makes you a winner! He is in front, blocking and knocking things out of the way for you. Just stay behind him and continue to move forward!

You are blessed to be a Blessing!

*My prayer for you today is that you will ask God for
wisdom and understanding so that He will make
you the success that you know you can be!*

Your scripture for today:

Colossians 3:23-24

**Whatever you do, work at it with all your heart, as
working for the Lord, not for men, since you know
that you will receive an inheritance from the Lord as
a reward. It is the Lord Christ you are serving.**

Observation:

*You must recognize that God is in everyone, even the people you work
for. Sometimes it may be hard to see, but you have to look with your
spiritual eyes. Look past the surface of things and understand that
God is your rewarder. Before you start your work day you can pray
for those you work with and for. You can bless the work environment
you are in every day. You can pray for everyone you come in contact
with and pray for peace in our work place. Then devote your work day
to the Lord!*

You are blessed to be a Blessing!

> *My prayer for you today is that you will work all
> things as onto the Lord. He will give you the grace
> to do it and bless you at the same time!*

December 20

Your scripture for today:

Ephesians 1:3

Praise be to the God and Father of our Lord Jesus Christ, who has blessed us in the heavenly realms with every spiritual blessing in Christ.

Observation:

There is no need to wonder if God will bless you because he has already stored up the blessings in heaven to get to you when you are ready to receive them. Don't put limits on your dreams. Dream big and ask God to bless the work of your hands and give you the strength to get up each day. Can you imagine God's store room of blessings? I imagine it would have everything you could think of and asked for there with your name on it. You have your own area of blessings because He knows what you dream of having and what you have thought about wanting in your life. It's all there and waiting on you to claim it. Make sure you get in tune with God and build up your faith muscle. When you ask God for anything, believe that you already received it and you will have it. It's right there in the store room of blessings just waiting on you. So when you receive it, thank God for it and believe that there is more where it came from. Seek first the kingdom of God and his righteousness and all these things will be added on to you.

You are blessed to be a Blessing!

My prayer for you today is that you will ask for what you want and God will bless you with it as long as you are ready to receive it! So GET READY!

December 21

Your scripture for today:

James 3:17-18

**But the wisdom that comes from heaven is first of all
pure; then peace-loving, considerate, submissive, full of
mercy and good fruit, impartial and sincere. Peacemakers
who sow in peace reap a harvest of righteousness.**

Observation:

*There are times that we go to others for advice and this scripture
gives us a check list to know if the advice you are receiving is from
heaven. First of all is it pure? You want to make sure that the advice
isn't mixed with anything and it's not harmful. Then ask yourself is
it peace-loving? Will this advice bring peace to the situation? Is the
advice considerate? Does this advice consider others feelings or how it
will affect someone else? Does that advice submit to those in authority?
Make sure that the advice is forgiving and will not harbor any ill
feeling and will produce good feelings. Make sure that when you take
advice or ask for wisdom from anyone that it is has all the qualities of
the wisdom that comes from heaven!*

You are blessed to be a Blessing!

*My prayer for you today is that you will seek wisdom that
exemplifies the qualities of the wisdom that comes from heaven!*

December 22

Your scripture for today:

Numbers 6:24-26

**"The LORD bless you
and keep you;
the LORD make his face shine on you
and be gracious to you;
the LORD turn his face toward you
and give you peace."**

Observation:

This is a powerful way to bless others as the Lord instructed Aaron to bless the Israelites. When you take the time to speak a blessing over someone else God will turn around and bless you too. This prayer says it all. You are asking God to bless them and keep them in His protective arms. And while He is doing that give them grace which is Gods unmerited favor, which will allow them to do everything with ease. Then to ask God to always be attentive to them by turning his face toward them and giving them the peace of God that passes all understanding. This is an amazing prayer to pray for yourself and for your loved ones!

You are blessed to be a Blessing!

*My prayer for you today:
May the Lord bless you and keep you; May the Lord make his face shine on you and be gracious to you; May the Lord turn his face toward you and give you his peace! Amen*

December 23

Your scripture for today:

Matthew 1:20-21

But after he had considered this, an angel of the Lord appeared to him in a dream and said, "Joseph son of David, do not be afraid to take Mary home as your wife, because what is conceived in her is from the Holy Spirit. She will give birth to a son, and you are to give him the name Jesus, because he will save his people from their sins."

Observation:

There are times when the things that are happening in our life are unbelievable. You sit back and wonder why this is happening to me? You have done everything right, stayed out of trouble and now this! I imagine that is how Joseph must have felt when all of a sudden Mary is pregnant. That is why an angel had to appear to Joseph to comfort him not to be afraid. Just know that the Lord is aware of everything you are facing. He has already established your deliverance and the blessing that will be birthed from the situation. Keep your faith and know that God's got it all under control!

You are blessed to be a Blessing!

> *My prayer for you today is that you will always know that God's got it all under control! Don't be afraid!*

Your scripture for today:

Luke 1:41-42

When Elizabeth heard Mary's greeting, the baby leaped in her womb, and Elizabeth was filled with the Holy Spirit. In a loud voice she exclaimed: "Blessed are you among women, and blessed is the child you will bear!

Observation:

Have you ever connected with someone who has the same or similar dreams and goals? You are able to talk for hours and relate to so many things. There is so much power in that interaction because you are able to encourage each other to do what it is that God has placed inside of you to do. I have a friend like that, every time we go to lunch we get to talking about her business or my business and the creative ideas start flowing and you know that it's a God thing. Make sure that you surround yourself with people that will lift your spirits and make your insides jump with excitement. You can also be an encourager and bless others with your words. When you think about the awesome gift that Mary was about to birth into the world she could have had much fear! But God sent an angel to her to tell her not to be afraid! That baby or dream you have been carrying around needs to be birthed. It's going to help so many people you don't have to be afraid!

You are blessed to be a Blessing!

My prayer for you today is that you will birth the baby that God has placed in you as a dream. It's your time to bless the world with it!

December 25

Your scripture for today:

Isaiah 9:6

**For to us a child is born,
to us a son is given,
and the government will be on his shoulders.
And he is will be called
Wonderful Counselor, Mighty God,
Everlasting Father, and Prince of Peace.**

Observation:

Isn't it amazing that God gave Isaiah this prophecy so many years before it actually happened. I believe that God gives us visions for our future through dreams and desires that we have. You may think that you thought it up all by yourself but it was already ordained by God before you were formed in your Mother's womb. We all have to get to the point in our spiritual growth to recognize that it's God that places the desire in our hearts so that we can fulfill the purpose he put you here for. So on this day every year we celebrate the birth of our Lord and Savior Jesus Christ all over the world. He is our Wonderful Counselor, Mighty God, Everlasting Father and our Prince of Peace! Happy Birthday Jesus!

You are blessed to be a Blessing!

*My prayer for you today is praise God for sacrificing His son
and sending him to us to deliver us and save us! Thanks,
glory, honor, and praise belong to you and you alone!*

Your scripture for today:

Ephesians 3:20

Now to Him who is able to do exceedingly abundantly above all that we ask or think, according to the power that works in us, to Him be glory...

Observation:

When someone goes above and beyond something you asked them to do you are so excited. It shows that they really heard and listened to your request. But they took the information then added more to it then you even thought they would do. When you are in a customer service role and you treat your customer this way you get great tips and the customer will always come to you. That's how God is with us. He is not just able to do beyond what we ask, but abundantly beyond. But that's not enough, He is able to do exceedingly abundantly beyond what we ask. Now, what is it that you need? Build up your faith so that God can work with the power within you to make it come to pass. Get outrageous with your faith and ask God to do far beyond what you can think. We have not because we ask not! Just make sure to give Him the glory, honor and praise!

You are blessed to be a Blessing!

> *My prayer for you today is that you will know that God is willing and able to do more for you than your mind can conceive. If he were to tell you it would blow your mind! Just ask and you will receive over and above what you can think!*

December 27

Your scripture for today:

2 Chronicles 14:11

Then Asa called to the Lord his God and said, "Lord, there is no one like you to help the powerless against the mighty. Help us, Lord our God, for we rely on you, and in your name we have come against this vast army. Lord, you are our God; do not let mere mortals prevail against you."

Observation:

When you know who to call on in times of trouble you will win every time! God will fight your battles for you, all you have to do is ask Him, rely on Him and believe that He already has done it for you! You are never powerless when you have the mighty hand of God available to you. When it seems that so much is coming against you and your problems are over your head just remember that it's under God's feet! Nothing's too hard or too big that God can't handle for you! Think about it from God's point of view. He can see the full picture of the situation from beginning to the end. He knows who you need to know to make things work for you. He has already given you the favor and grace to get through it. Believe it, declare it, and God will prove it to you!

You are blessed to be a Blessing!

> *My prayer for you today is that you will understand that you have the power of God at your disposal. You will always win when you call on the Master!*

December 28

Your scripture for today:

Nehemiah 13:14

Remember me, O my God, for this. Don't ever forget the devoted work I have done for The Temple of God and its worship.

Observation:

We all want to be remembered for what we do. When you are recognized for your service it inspires you to do more because you feel appreciated! You may faithfully serve in your church or devote your time to a charity. God remembers you and is always reminded of you because the people you are serving are thanking Him for you. He is constantly hearing your name! Be encouraged today and know that your service is not in vain! God sees the work and time you put in to serve others. He is pleased with you and even though much of what you do is done in secret. God will reward you in public for all to see the goodness of the Lord in the land of the living!

You are blessed to be a Blessing!

My prayer for you today is that you will know that God sees all that you do and will reward you with many abundant blessings!

December 29

Your scripture for today:

Joshua 1:5-6

No one will be able to stand against you all the days of your life. As I was with Moses, so I will be with you; I will never leave you nor forsake you. Be strong and courageous, because you will lead these people to inherit the land I swore to their ancestors to give them.

Observation:

When you are called to be a leader you need to be encouraged to step up and be strong. Leaders can face opposition, criticism, and defiance from those that they have been chosen to lead. But when God has given a vision He also gives you the provision to do it. Look at all that Moses went through and all he was doing was obeying the assignment that God had given him. You have to be strong and courageous to withstand all that may come against you. Don't look to the right or the left. Stay with it and you and your people will inherit what God has promised you!

You are blessed to be a Blessing!

My prayer for you today is that you will lead with the courage and strength that God has given you!

December 30

Your scripture for today:

Haggai 2:9

The glory of this present house will be greater than the glory of the former house,' says the Lord Almighty. 'And in this place I will grant peace,' declares the Lord Almighty."

Observation:

As you move into the promises that God has for you the enemy will try to stop you from obtaining the best that God has for you! He will use devious tactics, discouragement, depression, and even the people you think are your friends to get you off track. When God moves you to a new place in life He is setting you up for greater victories. You have to hold on and be strong in the Lord and the power of his might. This year has passed and you are still here so that means God still has things for you to do. When He closes one door he will open another one bigger and better than the previous. You will be abundantly blessed and most of all receive the peace of God that passes all understanding.

You are blessed to be a Blessing!

My prayer for you today is that you look to God to move you to His place of abundance! That's where you will find peace and prosperity!

Your scripture for today:

Joel 2:25-26

I will repay you for the years the locusts have eaten the great locust and the young locust, the other locust and locust swarm my great army that I sent among you. You will have plenty to eat, until you are full, and you will praise the name of the Lord your God, who has worked wonders for you: never again will my people be shamed.

Observation:

God wants to restore you! He is in the restoration business, so what you need, He's got it! We're coming into a new year of new beginnings and God is going to repay back to you double for your trouble, so give glory to God. Think of anything you can give thanks for and with that attitude of gratitude begin to give God thanks. No matter how small it may seem God can bless that! Those who are thankful are fruitful and those who are thankless are fruitless. Let's begin this New Year with thanksgiving in our hearts and praise in our mouths! The past is over all things have become new!

You are blessed to be a Blessing!

My prayer for you today is that you will look to the New Year with a new set of eyes. See it from God's perspective knowing that he is able to make all things new in your life.

Conclusion

I want to thank you for reading Your Scripture For Today. My hope is that it has blessed your life because I know it has blessed me as I have been writing it. I pray that you will continue to look back and read the scriptures every day making it a daily practice. You are important in the kingdom of God and He wants you to get to know who he is and how he operates. As you continue to grow in the spirit realm you will increase your faith and see miracles happen every day. Remember to keep an attitude of gratitude and you will prosper. God continues to amaze me with His goodness, grace, peace, mercy and favor! My wish is that you will experience the best that only God can give you as you realize that your best is still yet to come!

You truly are

BLESSED TO BE A BLESSING!

Works Cited

Bible References

- *New International Version (NIV)* - THE HOLY BIBLE, NEW INTERNATIONAL VERSION®, NIV® Copyright © 1973, 1978, 1984, 2011 by Biblica, Inc.® Used by permission. All rights reserved worldwide.

- *The Message* - *The Message.* Copyright © 1993, 1994, 1995, 1996, 2000, 2001, 2002. Used by permission of NavPress Publishing Group."

- *English Standard Version* - The ESV® Bible (The Holy Bible, English Standard Version®) copyright © 2001 by Crossway, a publishing ministry of Good News Publishers. ESV® Text Edition: 2011. The ESV® text has been reproduced in cooperation with and by permission of Good News Publishers. All rights reserved.

- *The Amplified Bible* - The "Amplified" trademark is registered in the United States Patent and Trademark Office by The Lockman Foundation. Use of this trademark requires the permission of The Lockman Foundation.

Internet Website Used

- *Bible Gateway* - https://www.**biblegateway**.com

Printed in the United States
By Bookmasters